THE Double Diamond PRINCIPLE

58 SUCCESS SECRETS IN THE LIFE OF JESUS

BY MIKE MURDOCK

Wisdom is the principal t⸻ ⸻d with thy all gett⸻

D1059225

Wisdom Training Center
P. O. Box 99
Dallas, Texas 75221

Unless otherwise indicated, all Scripture quotations are taken from the *King James Version* of the Bible.

The Double Diamond Principle
ISBN 1-56394-000-0
Copyright © 1990 by Mike Murdock
P. O. Box 99
Dallas, Texas 75221

Published by
Wisdom International
P. O. Box 747
Dallas, Texas 75221

Printed in the United States of America. All rights reserved under International Copyright Law. Contents and/or cover may not be reproduced in whole or in part in any form without the expressed written consent of the Publisher.

FOREWORD

I've known Mike Murdock for a number of years. I've been captivated by his teaching. I've been inspired by his songs. I've read and reread his writings. Most of all, I have enjoyed his emphasis on being a WINNER.

WINNING is the focus of this book, *The Double Diamond Principle.* In it, you will find 58 Master Secrets for Total Success--Double-Diamond Principles that are tailor-made for anyone who wants to build a foundation upon Christ's Wisdom.

After reading Mike's book, I am more convinced than ever that if we follow our Master's example, we can reach our greatest goals and achieve our most cherished dreams.

Let me offer three quick examples from the book:

In Master Secret 9, Mike explores the sometimes-controversial topic of finances. He writes,

"These are the facts: Jesus showed people *where* money could be found. He *motivated* them to try again and consider options and changes. He focused their minds on the *True Source,* the heavenly Father. He encouraged them to make *spiritual* matters a priority. Then He encouraged them to look at their giving as a Seed, linked to a *100-fold harvest.* He encouraged them to *expect a harvest* from everything they sowed into others and into God's work."

In Master Secret 41, you are shown how to unlock the much-needed guideline of completing whatever you start. I especially like Mike's sentence, "Champions are finishers." It quickly becomes evident--from the scriptures and stories which are detailed--that Jesus was the greatest Finisher of all time.

Master Secret 56 points toward the example of seeking mentorship. Jesus outlined this principle numerous times for His followers. Mike offers this challenge:

"Show me your mentors, and I can predict your future."

I could go on and on about the wonderful nuggets of eternal truth you will find in this book, but I don't want to delay you from starting your own gold-mining adventure through the pages which follow.

Suffice it to say that I heartily endorse *The Double-Diamond Principle*. It's one of Mike Murdock's best works. In these paragraphs, you will discover the principles for building your business and enriching your life.

More importantly, you will see, perhaps more clearly than ever before, how wonderful and extraordinary Jesus Christ was, is and shall be. As a result, your business and life will never be the same.

--Dexter R. Yager, Sr.
 Financial, business and
 marketing consultant

WHY I WROTE THIS BOOK

He was extremely excited. Even though he was telephoning me one thousand miles away, I sensed the incredible energy in his voice.

"Mike, how would you like to make one hundred thousand dollars a year for the rest of your life?" To many people that may not sound like a lot of money. But when you have just stepped out of a court room with lawyer bills stacked high, a costly divorce, and you do not even have enough money to buy a sofa, well one hundred thousand dollars a year sounds pretty good.

"What do you think!", I replied laughingly. He knew I would be interested. He was a precious man that I had admired for several years. He was also the pastor of a vibrant church of four thousand people. I had spoken there several times.

Within fourteen days, he had flown to Los Angeles where I was living at the time. He explained to me the multilevel marketing plan of the Amway organization. He explained that it was basically a business where you could purchase everyday items such as shampoo, washing detergent and other personal items. Then, it was important for you to share this with your friends who would also purchase these items through you, the distributor. He explained that when you signed up six friends who reached a certain level of sales within one month, they would be know as direct distributors.

"What happens when I help six other people become direct distributors at a certain level of sales?" I asked, rather doubtfully.

"*You become a Diamond.* That is a level that is considered extremely high status...almost the very highest, in the company," he explained.

"Is that the highest status that I can achieve? Or can I help more than six people reach that level of sales?"

He replied, "That is what is so wonderful about this business. The sky is the limit. You can sign as many people as you would like. When six of your people 'go direct', you will become a Diamond."

"What happens if I helped twelve people become direct distributors, instead of six?"

"You would then become a Double-Diamond."

Something excited my heart.

"That means that *Jesus was a Double-Diamond* Himself, wasn't He!" I laughed. He liked the comparison, and we continued to talk about the business.

As I learned about the business, and began to speak at various rallies, I saw some remarkable and beautiful things. I saw people striving to achieve something significant with their lives. Families coming together and focusing on financial freedom. I observed an insatiable appetite for knowledge and companionship in the business.

But, I saw something else quite startling.

I began to see an astounding collection of success secrets. They were actually in a book called the Holy Bible. They were almost hidden in the life of the *greatest man that ever lived, Jesus Christ.*

I had joked to a friend, *"Jesus Was A Double-Diamond.* He signed up twelve disciples and shook the earth with those twelve people. He was the master networker." But, the more I thought about it, the more I began to see that the Bible was literally a handbook on success and achievement on earth.

This book is for achievers.

This book is for dreamers.

This book is for champions.

This book is for those who feel like losers, but want to accomplish something extraordinary with their lives.

This book is about Jesus of Nazareth, and how His life reshaped the human race. He did it by influencing twelve men. Those twelve men influenced hundreds, who affected thousands, who influenced millions.

Jesus was the first Double-Diamond.

I have written this book to honor Him and His remarkable secrets that He left so visible for us on the pages of the scriptures.

That's why I wrote this book.

Dr. Mike Murdock

ONE SOLITARY LIFE

He was born in an obscure village. He worked in a carpenter's shop until He was thirty. He then became an itinerant preacher. He never held office. He never had a family or owned a house. He did not go to college. He had no credentials but Himself. He was only thirty three when the public turned against Him. His friends ran away. He was turned over to His enemies and went through the mockery of a trial. He was nailed to a cross between two thieves. While He was dying, His executioners gambled for His clothing, the only property He had on earth. He was laid in a borrowed grave.

Nineteen centuries have come and gone, and today He is the central figure of the human race. All the armies that ever marched, all the navies that ever sailed, all the parliaments that ever sat, and all the kings that ever reigned have not affected the life of man on earth as much as that **ONE SOLITARY LIFE.**

TABLE OF CONTENTS

JESUS HAD SOMETHING OTHERS NEEDED.

Everyone has problems.

Your success and happiness in life depends on your willingness to help someone solve their problem. *Successful people are simply problem solvers.* A successful attorney solves *legal* problems. Doctors solve *physical* problems. The automobile mechanic solves car problems.

Jesus was a Problem-Solver.

Thousands were burdened with guilt because of their sins. Jesus offered *forgiveness.* Thousands were spiritually starved. He said, "I am the Bread of Life." Hundreds had bodies riddled with sickness and disease. Jesus "went about doing good, and healing all that were sick and oppressed of the devil." *(Acts 10:38)* Many were possessed with evil spirits. Jesus set them *free.*

Jesus had something others needed.

He solved their problems. That's why thousands sat for days as He taught them concerning the laws of God and how to have extraordinary relationships with other people.

His products were boldy declared. Eternal life. Joy. Inner peace. Forgiveness. Healing and health. Financial freedom. Take an inventory of yourself. What do you have to offer someone? What do you *enjoy* doing? What would you attempt to do if you knew it was impossible to fail?

Double-Diamond Principle

Everything God Created Is A Solution To A Problem.

You are not an accident. God planned your birth. "Before I formed thee in the belly I knew thee; and before thou camest forth out of the womb I sanctified thee, and I ordained thee." *(Jeremiah 1:5)*

Everything God makes is a solution to a problem. Every person God created is a solution to a problem. God wanted a love relationship.

He created Adam. Adam was lonely. So, God created Eve. This is the golden thread that *links* creation.

Think of your *contribution* to another as an *assignment* from God. A lawyer is *assigned* to his client. A wife is *assigned* to her husband. Parents are *assigned* to their children. A secretary is *assigned* to her boss.

Your assignment is always to a person or a people.

For example, Moses was assigned to the Israelites. Aaron was assigned to Moses.

Your assignment will always *solve a problem.*

So, your life is a solution to someone in trouble. Find those who need you and what you have to offer. Build your life around that contribution.

Jesus did.

That is why He was a Double-Diamond.

JESUS BELIEVED IN HIS PRODUCT.

Doubt is deadly.

Have you ever walked into a room and felt anger in the atmosphere? Have you ever walked into a room and felt love and energy and excitement? Of course. *Your thoughts have presence.* They are like currents moving through the air. Those thoughts are capable of *drawing people toward us, or driving people away from us.*

Your attitude is always sensed. You will never succeed in any business unless you really believe in that business. You must believe in the product you are promoting. *Your doubts will eventually surface.*

Look at the life of Jesus. He believed He could *change* people. He believed that His product would *satisfy* people. "Whosoever drinketh of this water shall thirst again: But whosoever drinketh of the water that I shall give him shall never thirst; but the water that I shall give him shall be in him a well of water springing up into everlasting life." *(John 4:13-14)*

What makes you believe in your product? Product knowledge.

His product was life. "The thief cometh not, but for to steal, and to kill, and to destroy: I am come that they might have life, and that they might have it more abundantly." *(John 10:10)*

Double-Diamond Principle

Whatever You Have Been Given Is What Someone Needs.

He saw the damaged products. He knew that He was their connection for repair. Nobody could take His place and He knew it. "My sheep hear my voice and I know them, and they follow me." *(John 10:27)*

You must take the time and make the effort to *know your product.* It may bore you, or even seem unnecessary. You may be anxious to sell your product. *But success just does not happen that way.*

A lawyer must study new laws. A doctor must keep well-read on the latest journals concerning the body and new diseases. A policeman has to study his weapons, the laws of his community, his rights and the mind-set of criminals. If he does not study this, he knows he is "a dead man in the streets." His life is on the line.

Information Breeds Confidence.

Don't expect to succeed unless you are thoroughly informed about your product.

Are you discouraged by your present job? Are you feeling a bit hopeless? Then, I suggest that you ask yourself some real soul-searching and honest questions. How much *time* have you spent cultivating an awareness of your business? Do you *use* your product? How many hours each day have you *invested* in *becoming informed?* Are you so busy trying to "make a buck" that you really have not developed a powerful understanding and confidence in what you are doing?

Jesus was very busy. He was teaching, preaching, traveling, performing miracles, and mentoring the unlearned. But, He always took the time to get alone with His Father and renew His understanding of His Purpose, His Plan, and His

Product. "My people are destroyed for lack of knowledge."
(Hosea 4:6)

Jesus believed in His product.

That is why He was a Double-Diamond.

JESUS NEVER MISREPRESENTED HIS PRODUCT.

Liars are eventually exposed.

It may take weeks or even months, but the truth always surfaces. "He that covereth his sins shall not prosper." *(Proverbs 28:13)*

Anyone who does business with you wants the truth. The total truth. People fear misrepresentation.

Jesus had the greatest product on earth: salvation. He offered the human race an opportunity to have a relationship with God. He spoke of heaven and angels. "In my Father's house are many mansions: if it were not so, I would have told you." *(John 14:2)*

But, He never painted a distorted picture.

He warned His disciples of *persecution.* "But beware of men: for they will deliver you up to the councils, and they will scourge you in their synagogues." *(Matthew 10:17)*

He spoke of their *afflictions.* "Then shall they deliver you up to be afflicted, and shall kill you: and ye shall be hated of all nations for my name's sake." *(Matthew 24:9)*

He spoke of *loneliness.* "The foxes have holes, and the birds of the air have nests; but the Son of man hath not where to lay his head." *(Matthew 8:20)*

Double-Diamond Principle

Give Another What He Cannot Find Anywhere Else, And He Will Keep Returning.

Jesus believed in preparing people for any possible situation that could happen. He was honest. His teaching was far more than a "pie in the sky" philosophy.

Listen to the Apostle Paul.   "Of the Jews five times received I forty stripes save one. Thrice was I beaten with rods, once I was stoned, thrice I suffered shipwreck, a night and a day I have been in the deep." *(II Corinthians 11:24,25)*

This certainly does not sound like the most ideal sales talk to a group of students in Bible School. Paul did not misrepresent his product either.

Jesus spoke to many people of the good things and the benefits of what He offered. But, He was also quick to talk to them about the *total* picture, so they would be prepared to face their trials.

Address the benefits. Focus on the advantages that your product or your business will offer to another person. But never forget *that an honest relationship is worth one hundred sales.*

Your integrity will always be remembered longer than your product.

Jesus was honest.

That is why He was a Double-Diamond.

JESUS WENT WHERE THE PEOPLE WERE.

Somebody needs you.

Go find them. Activate yourself. Move toward neighbors. Move toward the members of your family. Get on the telephone. Go ahead, write that brief note to that close friend. You may be shy, timid and even feel inadequate. But, you will not succeed in life unless you are connected to people.

Success involves people. People who enable you to succeed may not always come to you. In fact, they rarely do. *You must go to them.*

Why do you think there are newspaper machines on every corner, and soft drink machines are on every floor of a hotel?

Successful people are accessible.

You will never possess what you are unwilling to pursue.

Jesus knew this. He did not set up a throne in the middle of each city and say, "This is my palace. This is the only place you can see me." He went to the marketplace. He went to the boats of fishermen. He went to the synagogue. He went to the homes of the people. He went everywhere. He "went through the towns preaching the gospel and healing every where." *(Luke 9:6)*

He was reachable.

Double-Diamond Principle

**You Will Never Possess
What You Are Unwilling To Pursue.**

What is keeping you from reaching out toward others? Is it an inward fear or dread that you may be rejected or turned down? Are you intimidated in some way? There is something far more important than any rejection: *Your dreams and goals.*

Successful people are reachers. They dread rejection, too. But, they believe their goal is worth it.

Jesus left comfort. He left the presence of angels and His heavenly Father. He willingly walked into an atmosphere that was unholy and imperfect. He stepped out of a magnificent and perfect kingdom and into a world that was confused, stained and deadly. But, He walked *into* the lives of those who needed Him.

He went where the people were.

Your dream is connected to people. Lawyers need clients. Doctors need patients. Singers need musicians. Salesmen need customers.

Jesus went where people were hurting. He went to the lame, the blind, the poor, the wealthy. He talked to the learned, the ignorant, the hungry, the thirsty.

So, *start your People-List today.* There are two kinds of people in your life: 1) Those who already know that you have something they need, and 2) Those who do not yet know you have something they need.

Your People-List may include your relatives. Neighbors. Newspaper boy. Gardener. Dentist. Manicurist. Hairdresser. Landlord. Doctor. Lawyer.

There is a *Law of Relationship* that says every person is merely four people away from any other human on earth. Think of it! This simply means that you know Bill, who knows Judy, who knows Charles, who knows anyone else you would ever want to know. *You are already networked with the entire world.*

You simply have to get out of your house. Get out of your car. Go to the door. Reach for your telephone.

Success always begins somewhere.
Success always begins at some moment.
Success always begins with someone.
You must go where people are.
Jesus did.
That is why He was a Double-Diamond.

JESUS TOOK TIME TO REST.

Fatigue can be costly.

One notable President of the United States knew this. He absolutely refused to make any major decision after 4:00 in the afternoon. He knew that a *tired mind rarely makes good decisions.*

One bad decision can create countless tragedies.

Rest and recreation are not a sin. Rest time is *repair* time. It is *not* a loss of productivity. It is time for *renewing.* It is *receiving time.* It helps *release* your potential.

Jesus was an action man. A people person. He produced. He healed. He preached and taught. He walked among the people. *But He also knew the necessity of rest and relaxation.* "Come ye yourselves apart into a desert place, and rest a while:" (Mark 6:31)

Think about this. Daily, He faced hundreds of the sick and afflicted who screamed for His attention. Many were demon possessed. Mothers reached for Him. Fathers asked Him to pray for their children. Children did not want to leave His presence.

But, He *separated* Himself...*to receive.*

He knew that He could only give away that which He possessed. Work time is *giving.* Rest time is *receiving.* You must have both.

God created the earth in six days. But, He took the time to *rest* on the seventh day. He set an example for us. *Jesus did the same thing.*

Double-Diamond
Principle

Faith Walks Out,
When Fatigue Walks In.

That might be the reason He was able to accomplish so much in three and a half years.

Life is demanding. People are demanding. In fact, the more you succeed, the more people will demand of you.

It is up to you to repair yourself.

Work hard. But, play just as enthusiastically. *Schedule it.* Take one day a week off completely. Totally relax. Focus on something completely different than your job. Your mind will think clearer. You will make better decisions. You will see life through different eyes. You will accomplish far more in less time.

Stop your frantic push for success. Take time to *taste the present.* The fires of desire will *always* rage within you. You must dominate that rage and focus on it. *Learn to rest.*

Jesus did.

That is why He was a Double-Diamond.

JESUS TOOK TIME TO PLAN.

Champions plan.

Planning is the starting point for any dream or goal that you possess.

What is a plan? A plan is *a written list of arranged actions* necessary to achieve your desired goal. "Write the vision, and make it plain upon tables, that he may run that readeth it." *(Habakkuk 2:2)*

Jesus planned your future. "In my Father's house are many mansions: if it were not so, I would have told you. I go to prepare a place for you." *(John 14:2)*

Think for a moment. God scheduled the birth, the crucifixion, and resurrection of His Son before the foundation of the earth. "And all that dwell upon the earth shall worship him, whose names are not written in the Book of Life of the Lamb slain from the foundation of the world." *(Revelation 13:8)*

I think it is quite fascinating that God would schedule a meal, the marriage supper, six thousand years ahead! "Blessed are they which are called unto the Marriage Supper of the Lamb." *(Revelation 19:9)*

Double-Diamond Principle

The Secret Of Your Future Is Hidden In Your Daily Routine.

God always honored men who planned.

Noah *planned* the building of the ark. Solomon, the wisest man who ever lived on earth, *took time to plan* the building of the temple. Moses, the great deliverer, who brought the Israelites out of Egypt *took time to plan* the tabernacle.

Your Bible is the *plan of God* for you, the world, and eternity. It is the undeniable proof that God thinks ahead. Most of the Bible is prophecy, a description of the future before it ever occurs.

Jesus taught, "For which of you, intending to build a tower, sitteth not down first, and counteth the cost, whether he have sufficient to finish it? Lest haply, after he hath laid the foundation, and is not able to finish it, all that behold it begin to mock him, Saying, This man began to build, and was not able to finish. Or what king, going to make war against another king, sitteth not down first, and consulteth whether he be able with ten thousand to meet him that cometh against him with twenty thousand?" *(Luke 14:28-31)*

Make a list of things to do every day of your life. Write six things you want to accomplish, that day. Focus your total attention on each task. Assign each task to a specific time. (If you cannot plan events for twenty-four hours in your life, what makes you think you will accomplish your desires for the next twenty-four years?)

Think of each hour as an employee. *Delegate a specific assignment to each hour.* What do you want to accomplish between 7 o'clock A.M. and 9 o'clock A.M.? Who should you telephone today?

Write out your plan clearly on a sheet of paper. *Successes are usually scheduled events.* Failures are not.

Planning is laborious. It is tedious. It is meticulous. It is grilling, demanding and exhausting. In my personal opinion, detailed planning is really never fun. *But sometimes you have to do something you hate to create something you love.*

Why do people avoid planning? Some avoid it because it is time consuming. They are so busy "mopping up the water" that they do not take the time to turn off the faucet!

The secret of your future is hidden in your daily routine.

Even ants think ahead. "Go to the ant, thou sluggard; consider her ways, and be wise: Which having no guide, overseer, or ruler, Provideth her meat in the summer, and gathered her food in the harvest." *(Proverbs 6:6-8)*

Jesus had a plan.

That is why He was a Double-Diamond.

JESUS KNEW THAT HE DID NOT HAVE TO CLOSE EVERY SALE TO BE A SUCCESS.

No simply means to "ask again."

Stop for a moment. Review your past experiences. You encountered rejection when you were a child. Some of your school mates may not have liked you. But you made it anyway, didn't you?

Rejection is not fatal. It is merely someone's opinion.

Jesus experienced more rejection than any human who ever lived on earth. He was born in a stable. He was born as an outcast in society. (Even today, television talk show hosts belittle and make fun of Him and those who follow Him. The name of Jesus is used daily as a curse word by millions. His own people rejected him.)

"He came unto his own, and his own received him not." *(John 1:11)*

Did He quit? When Judas betrayed Him, did He allow Himself to become demoralized? No. *Jesus knew that He did not have to close every sale to be a success.* He went on to the others, who discerned His value. "But as many as received him, to them gave he power to become the sons of God, even to them that believe on his name." *(John 1:12)* He knew His *worth.* He knew His *product.*

Double-Diamond Principle

**Double-Diamonds Do Things They Hate
To Create Something They Love.**

He knew that critics died, but His plan was eternal.

Jesus was willing to experience a *season of pain,* to create an *eternity of gain. Some things last longer than rejection.* Your goals and dreams.

Move beyond your scars. Not everyone will celebrate you. Not everyone will welcome your future.

Someone needs what you have. Your contribution is an absolute necessity for their success. Discern it.

Pharisees rejected Jesus. The religious sect called Sadducees rejected Him. Religious leaders despised Christ. Those who should have recognized His worth wanted to destroy Him.

Jesus risked rejection to become the golden link between man and God.

Babe Ruth was famous for many years as the home run king in baseball history. Many people have never realized that he had more strike outs than any other batter also! They have not remembered his losses at bat. They merely remember his successes. He was willing to risk a strike out to hit that home run.

Most great salesmen say that knowing that fourteen out of fifteen people will say no, merely inspires them to hurry and make their presentations to as many as possible, to reach that one who will accept.

Jesus taught His disciples how to handle rejection. "And whosoever shall not receive you, nor hear your words, when ye depart out of that house or city, shake off the dust of your feet." *(Matthew 10:14)*

So, climb off your recliner. Make that telephone call. Write that letter.

Sooner or later you will succeed.

Jesus knew this.

That is why He was a Double-Diamond.

JESUS WAS A PROBLEM-SOLVER.

You were created to change somebody.

Every person you meet today is trying to *change* their life in some way. They desire excellence. They want *financial freedom.* They want their *health* to improve. They hate loneliness. You may not be sent to everyone, but you are definitely sent to someone.

You may not be qualified to help every person you meet. *But somebody needs something you possess.* It may be your warmth, your love, your gifts, or a special opportunity you can provide them.

Jesus understood this. He knew that He could *change* people for *good.* He possessed something that could eliminate sorrow and heartache from their life. He was a *Restorer.* He was a *Repairer.* "The thief cometh not, but for to steal, and to kill, and to destroy: I am come that they might have life, and that they might have it more abundantly." *(John 10:10)* Jesus understood the insatiable appetite for self-improvement and excellence.

Double-Diamond Principle

**You Can Only Conquer Your Past
By Focusing On Your Future.**

There are four kinds of people in your life: those who add, subtract, divide, or multiply. Every relationship will affect you. For good or bad. *Those who do not increase you inevitably will decrease you.* "He that walketh with wise men shall be wise: but a companion of fools shall be destroyed." *(Proverbs 13:20) Each relationship nurtures a strength or a weakness within you.*

Thousands of people want to *change*. They just don't know how to change. Every alcoholic hates his bondage. Most smokers long to quit. Drug addicts sit for hours wondering how they can break the chains of bondage.

Jesus looked for people in trouble. That's why He told His disciples that He needed to go through Samaria, where He met a woman with five marriages that had failed. He talked. She listened. He changed her life so permanently, that she went back into the city proclaiming the influence of Jesus in her life. *She conquered her past by focusing on her future.*

"But whosoever drinketh of the water that I shall give him shall never thirst; but the water that I shall give him shall be in him a well of water springing up into everlasting life." *(John 4:14)* Jesus was water to the *thirsty*. He was bread to the *hungry*. He was a road map to the *lost*. He was a companion to the *lonely*.

Stop for a moment. What are your own greatest gifts? What is the *center of your expertise?* Are you a *good listener?* A good *speaker?* Whatever your gift is, that is what God will use to bless others through you.

Joseph had the ability to interpret dreams. Ruth took care of Naomi.

Your gift may not be needed by everybody. But it is definitely needed by *somebody*. Who are they? What is your gift? Whose life are you capable of improving today? Whose income could you improve? Whose peace of mind could you affect?

You are capable of motivating *somebody*. Maybe you can provide a climate, an atmosphere that unlocks the creativity of another. People want to succeed. People want to improve.

Someone has been waiting for you for a lifetime. They are worth pursuing. You are the golden thread missing in their life.

People want to *change*.

Jesus knew this.

That is why He was a Double-Diamond.

JESUS WAS CONCERNED ABOUT PEOPLE'S FINANCES.

Money is a reward.

Money is what you receive *when you help someone else achieve their goal.*

Payday is simply reward day. You are rewarded for spending your best hours of each day, your energy, and knowledge in helping your boss. He paid you for enabling him to reach his goal.

Money is very important. You cannot live in your home without it. You cannot provide for your family without it. Your automobile costs money. Your clothes cost money. Most marriage counselors observe that the number one cause of divorce is financial conflict.

Jesus recognized the importance of money.

Some think Jesus was a wandering nomad who wore a dirty white robe and sandals and who lived off scraps of food in the villages He visited. To the contrary, He had twelve men who handled His business. One was the treasurer. *(John 13:29)*

Double-Diamond Principle

**Your Future Begins With
Whatever Is In Your Hands Today.**

Someone has said that Jesus talked more about money than heaven. In fact, twenty percent of His teaching and conversation was about talents, money and finances.

Jesus did not want you to worry about finances. "Therefore I say unto you, Take no thought for your life, what ye shall eat, or what ye shall drink; nor yet for your body, what ye shall put on. Is not the life more than meat, and the body than raiment? Behold the fowls of the air: for they sow not, neither do they reap, nor gather into barns; yet your heavenly Father feedeth them. Are ye not much better than they?" *(Matthew 6:25,26)*

Jesus knew that God loved to give people good things. "Every good gift and every perfect gift is from above, and cometh down from the Father." *(James 1:17)*

Money is a fact of life. It is necessary. You need it. Money is on God's mind. It is taught about in the Word of God.

God loves to see His people prosper. "Let the Lord be magnified, which hath pleasure in the prosperity of his servant." *(Psalms 35:27)*

God wants to reveal ways for you to profit and succeed financially. "I am the Lord thy God which teacheth thee to profit." *(Isaiah 48:17)*

Jesus showed people *how to get ahead financially*, through His parables about using your gifts and talents. *(Matthew 25:14-23)*

Your future starts with whatever is in your hand today. Nothing is too little to multiply. Everything is *reproductive.* Everyone has received something from God capable of reproducing.

Jesus showed people that God was their true Source of everything. *(Matthew 6:33)*

Jesus taught that giving was one of the ways to get ahead. "Give, and it shall be given unto you; good measure, pressed down, and shaken together, and running over, shall men give into your bosom. For with the same measure that ye mete withal it shall be measured to you again." *(Luke 6:38)*

Jesus taught the Law of Expectation that could unlock the 100-fold return. "But he shall receive an hundredfold now in this time, houses, and brethren, and sisters, and mothers, and children, and lands, with persecutions; and in the world to come eternal life." *(Mark 10:30)*

Jesus taught that you could give your way out of trouble. *(Luke 6:38)*

Jesus taught fishermen where to drop their nets to catch fish. *(Luke 5:1-10)*

Notice these incredible secrets: 1) Jesus visited people *where* they worked. 2) Jesus was so interested in their work that He instructed them as to the right time to drop their fishing nets and catch fish. 3) The disciples had enough confidence in Jesus' knowledge that they went ahead and dropped their nets again in total obedience. 4) They caught more fish than they had ever caught, so much that their net broke. 5) Their success was so remarkable they had to have partners to help them pull in the fish. 6) When the disciples saw the incredible knowledge and concern and results of following Jesus' instructions, they realized how sinful they were, how limited they were. 7) They brought their ships to land, and decided to totally follow Jesus and His teachings. *(Luke 5:11)*

Jesus took the time to show his disciples where to get money to pay their taxes. "Go thou to the sea, and cast an hook, and take up the fish that first cometh up; and when thou hast opened his mouth, thou shalt find a piece of money: that take, and give unto them for me and thee." *(Matthew 17:27)*

These are the facts: Jesus showed people *where* money could be found. He *motivated* them to *try* again and consider options and changes. He focused their mind on their *True Source*, the heavenly Father. He encouraged them to make *spiritual* matters a priority. Then, He encouraged them to look at their giving *as a seed*, linked to a *100-fold harvest*. He encouraged them to *expect a harvest* from everything they sowed into others and into God's work.

If there is one thing more exciting than "making money", *it is helping others discover financial freedom, too.*

Jesus did.

That is why He was a Double-Diamond.

34

JESUS WAS WILLING TO GO WHERE HE HAD NEVER BEEN BEFORE.

Geography makes a difference.

Pineapples do well in Hawaii. They do not do very well in Alaska. *Atmosphere matters.* The climate is important for any seed to grow.

You too, are a seed. Your business and your product are like seeds. It is true that you may need to change locations and situations to unlock the full potential of your success.

Success requires people. You will never succeed without networking with many different kinds of people. They may not be accessible. You may have to leave the comforts of your home to reach them to achieve extraordinary success.

Recently, I was amazed by what I saw in the life of Jesus. He was constantly in *movement,* constantly *changing* location.

"He was come down the mountain," *(Matthew 8:1)* "He entered into Capernaum..." *(8:5)* "He went to come into Peter's house..." *(8:14)* "He was entered into a ship..." *(8:23)* "And when He went into the country of the Gergesenes..." *(8:28)*

Double-Diamond Principle

You Must Be Willing To Go Where You Have Never Been, To Create Something You Have Never Had.

Jesus was constantly arising, departing, and going to new places. He sought to be around new people. He discussed His teaching with many types of people of varied backgrounds.

Some people will not come to where you are. You have to go to their home, their town and their environment.

Once, Jesus told His disciples to go to the upper room. They were to tarry there until they received the marvelous experience of the Holy Spirit. He told five hundred this. Three hundred eighty disobeyed Him. Even after they had observed His resurrection and His miracle life, only one hundred and twenty out of the five hundred actually followed His instruction. But, those who were willing to go to a different place...the Upper Room, received the marvelous outpouring of the Holy Spirit.

Abraham, the patriarch of the Israelites, had to make geographical changes before his success was birthed. *(Genesis 12:1,2)*

Joseph found his incredible success in *another country,* Egypt.

Ruth willingly left her heathen family in Moab, and went to Bethlehem with Naomi where she met Boaz, a financial giant of the community, and married him.

It is normal to move toward those who are easily accessible.

Sometimes you have to go somewhere you have never been before, before you taste the extraordinary success that you want to experience.

Jesus did.

That is why He was a Double-Diamond.

JESUS NEVER ALLOWED WHAT OTHERS SAID ABOUT HIM TO CHANGE HIS OPINION OF HIMSELF.

Nobody really knows you.

Consider this for a moment. Almost everyone in your life is more preoccupied with themselves than you. Therefore, you know more about yourself than anyone who will ever meet you. Never forget this.

It is not what men say about you that really matters in life. *It is what you believe about yourself.*

Jesus was slandered. He was falsely accused. They said He was possessed with devils. Countless accusations were hurled like stones against Jesus every day of His life. But, it never affected Him.

He knew what He was really about. He believed in Himself. He believed in His product. He knew that His accusers were ignorant, unlearned and arrogant. He knew they simply feared Him.

Double-Diamond Principle

The Ammunition Selected By Your Enemy Is A Clue To His Fear Of You.

People always fight what they do not understand. *The mind will always resent what it cannot master.* Wars are fought because of ignorance and fear. Throughout human history, champions have had their names soiled and stained. Accusations and slanderous lies have come against great political leaders as well as ministers. This is life. Daniel was accused of raping his empoyer's wife. Paul was accused of arousing mobs through hatred and division concerning their belief systems of religious people.

Jesus never begged anyone to believe in Him. He knew that *integrity cannot be proven, it must be discerned.*

He never wasted time with critics. He kept His attention on His goal. *He stayed focused.*

They accused Jesus of being filled with devils. He paid no attention. He simply continued to cast out devils. *(Matthew 12:24)*

Jesus never strived to "look good." *He simply was good.* He did not labor to appear truthful. *He was truthful.* He never struggled to have a good reputation. *He had character.*

**Integrity Cannot Be Proved,
It Must Be Discerned.**

Every successful man wants to be loved, admired. But, your enemies and critics will never leave your reputation unstained and untarnished. You must rise above that fact. You must never allow what others say about you to change your personal opinion of yourself. *Never.*

Jesus did not.

That is why He was a Double-Diamond.

JESUS UNDERSTOOD TIMING AND PREPARATION.

Champions never hurry.

The quality of preparation determines the quality of performance.

A great concert pianist invests hundreds of hours of practice before his concert. He knows that the quality of those many grueling hours of practice will prepare him for his greatest performance. The world champion heavyweight boxer knows that he cannot wait to get into the ring with his opponent to prepare. It would be too late. So, for many weeks before the great fight, he toils with his morning workout, running and exercise program.

Champions do not become *champions* in the ring. They are merely *recognized* in the ring. Their *becoming*, happens in their *daily routine*.

Jesus never hurried.

Jesus did not begin His earthly ministry until He was thirty years old. His ministry was a short three and one half years. *His preparation time was thirty years.*

Jesus was very sensitive about timing. When His mother told Him that the people had run out of wine at the marriage of Cana, He replied, "Woman what have I to do with thee? Mine hour is not yet come."

Jesus never hurried.

Double-Diamond Principle

Every Season Has A Product.

Several years ago, a friend of mine had just entered the Amway business. He was so excited about the remarkable potential of becoming a Diamond. However, he did not want to spend time in learning how to present the plan to others. He felt it was just "too detailed" to learn how to draw the circles. As I watched him stumble over and over in his conversations with others, I finally said, "Learn the business. Study the products. Take time to learn how to draw the circles. *If you will take the time to prepare, your presentation will have believability.* The people will have confidence in becoming a part of your business. You may not learn to draw circles the first night you hear about it, but don't worry, set aside some hours each week to begin to prepare your presentation."

Preparation time is never wasted time.

It will take time to know your business. It will take time to know your product. It will take time to develop a list of customers and clients.

Think about the life of Jesus. He saw hundreds die around Him because of sickness and disease. But His time had not come. He saw thousands warped with the traditions and legalism of religious systems. But He knew that His Father was growing Him up. "And Jesus increased in wisdom and stature, and in favour with God and man." (Luke 2:52) Jesus was willing to wait.

He *prepared* Himself.

This is why He was a Double-Diamond.

JESUS DEVELOPED A PASSION FOR HIS GOALS.

Passion is power.

You will never have significant success with anything *until it becomes an obsession with you.* An obsession is when something consumes your thoughts and time.

You will only be remembered in life for your obsession. Henry Ford, the automobile. Thomas Edison, inventions. Billy Graham, evangelism. Oral Roberts, healing. The Wright brothers, the airplane.

Jesus had a passion for His mission and goal in life. "For the Son of Man is come to seek and to save that which was lost." *(Luke 19:10)* "How God anointed Jesus of Nazareth with the Holy Ghost and with power: who went about doing good, d healing all that were oppressed of the devil; for God was with Him." *(Acts 10:38)*

Jesus focused on doing the exact instructions of His heavenly Father. He healed the sick. He noticed the lonely. He came to make people successful, to restore and repair their life to full fellowship with His Father.

Double-Diamond Principle

You Will Only Have Significant Success With Something That Is An Obsession.

That obsession took Him to the cross. It took Him to the crucifixion. Eight inches of thorns were crushed into His brow. A spear punctured His side. Spikes were driven into His hands. Thirty-nine stripes of a whip tore His back to shreds. Four hundred soldiers spit on His body. His beard was ripped off His face. But He was *obsessed with the salvation of mankind.*

And He succeeded.

You may start small. You may start with very little. But, if what you love begins to consume your mind, your thoughts, your conversation, your schedule, look for extraordinary success.

Do you dread going to work every morning? Do you anxiously look at the clock toward closing time each afternoon? Is your mind wandering throughout the day toward other places or things you would love to be doing? Then you will probably not have much success at what you are doing.

Find something that consumes you. Something that is worthy of building your entire life around. Consider it.

Jesus did.

That is why He was a Double-Diamond.

JESUS RESPECTED AUTHORITY.

Authority creates order.

Imagine a nation without a leader. A work place without a boss. An army without a General. Authority creates order, *the accurate arrangement of things.* (That is why you do not park your car in the bathroom!) You do not eat your meals in the garage! There is a place and a time for everything.

Respect those in authority over you. Your success is affected by it. Honor those who have lived before you. They possess a wealth of knowledge. Listen. Learn. Observe them.

Mentorship is the Master Key to extraordinary success.

Jesus understood this. He was the Son of God. He knew more than any other human on earth. Yet, He honored the authority of His own government. When people came to Him, questioning His opinion of paying taxes to Caesar, He answered, "Render to Caesar the things that are Caesar's, and to God the things that are God's." *(Mark 12:17)*

Are you speaking words of doubt about your own business? Are you belittling or criticizing your up-line? Stop it now. True, those in authority may not be perfect. They make mistakes. (Maybe that's why they can tolerate you! If they were perfect, they may not want to ever have any communication with you either!)

Double-Diamond
Principle

You Will Never Be Promoted Until You Become Over-Qualified For Your Present Position.

If you are rebelling against every instruction given to you, then do not complain when those around you begin to rebel against your words and opinions. Learn to honor and respect those in authority over you.

Jesus did.

That is why He was a Double-Diamond.

JESUS NEVER DISCRIMINATED.

Treat people right.

Some years ago, Elvis Presley did a concert in Indianapolis, Indiana. One of my close friends, a deputy sheriff, in Indianapolis, was in charge of security backstage. He noticed that a man was walking around dressed in an old windbreaker jacket. He was shuffling around as if he were some bum off the street. As my friend prepared to evict him from the building, someone stopped him and said, "That man is Colonel Parker, the manager of Elvis Presley." He was shocked and stunned. He had misjudged the man because of his appearance.

Stop prejudging people. Your first impression is always limited. It is possibly very wrong. *Only fools make permanent decisions without knowledge.* Never assume your intuition or perception is always correct.

Your success in business will be affected by prejudice, fear and any discrimination you allow.

Jesus never discriminated because of someone's race, sex or financial status.

He was comfortable in the presence of fishermen, or with the tax collectors of His day. He was at ease with men or women, the rich and the poor.

Double-Diamond Principle

Nobody Is Ever As They First Appear.

You see, *Jesus knew that everybody contained potential.* He never eliminated someone just because of their past. Born of a mother who conceived Him as a virgin, He knew what it meant to have a questionable background. He rose above it.

Jesus broke tradition. When the Samaritans were considered a lower class of people, and Jews would not even talk to them, Jesus did. In fact, He took the time to discuss with the woman at the well her entire life and *how He could change it.*

Peter said it this way, "Of a truth I perceive that God is no respecter of persons." *(Acts 10:34)*

James wrote it this way, "For if there come unto your assembly a man with a gold ring, in goodly apparel, and there come in also a poor man in vile raiment; And ye have respect to him that weareth the gay clothing, and say unto him, Sit thou here in a good place; and say to the poor, Stand thou there, or sit here under my footstool: Are ye not then partial in yourselves, and are become judges of evil thoughts?" *(James 2:2-4)*

Never eliminate anyone from the chain of your success.

Jesus refused to discriminate.

That is why He was a Double-Diamond.

JESUS OFFERED INCENTIVES.

Reward those who help you succeed.

People are motivated by two forces: Pain or pleasure. Fear or reward. Loss or gain.

For example, you may ask your child to mow the lawn. He sulks and complains, "But Daddy, I don't really want to mow the lawn today. I want to go play with my friends."

You have two ways to motivate him: pain or pleasure. Fear or incentive. Loss or gain. For instance, you may say, "Then son, bend over. I will have to discipline you with my belt." That is the *pain* motivation.

Or, you may use the *reward system.* "Son, I know you do not feel like doing it. But, if you do it, I will pay you $10." That is *incentive.* Reward. Gain.

Jesus used both methods to motivate.

In Luke 16, Jesus used fear motivation on the Pharisees who ridiculed Him. He described to them how the rich man went to hell and was "tormented in this flame."

However, when Jesus was talking to His disciples, He used *rewards and incentives* to motivate them. "In my Father's house are many mansions: if it were not so, I would have told you. I go to prepare a place for you." *(John 14:2,3)*

Double-Diamond Principle

You Will Always Move Toward Anyone Who Increases You and Away From Anyone Who Makes You Less.

You are created with a desire to *increase. Decrease is unnatural.* Remember, every person you meet today has an *appetite for increase.* They want to be benefited. There is nothing wrong with that. There is a God-given command on the inside of each person...to become more. *To multiply. (Genesis 1:28)*

Carefully examine the benefits that you offer to others. Who *needs* your product? *Why* do they need it? What *problem* will your product *solve in their life?* What do you offer others *that they cannot find anywhere else?*

Study the incentives of your present business. Know them "like the palm of your hand."

People never buy your product for the reasons *you* sell it. They buy products *for what it will do for them.*

David asked what rewards would come to him if he killed the giant Goliath. He was told simply that he would never have to pay taxes again, and he would be able to marry the king's daughter. He took five stones. He killed the giant. *He had motivation. He had an incentive.*

People do things for different reasons. Interrogate. Interview people. Ask questions. Find out what their greatest needs are. Dig to discover what their greatest fears may be.

Remember, you are there *to solve a problem.* Take the time to show others "what is in it for them." Make sure they understand the rewards and benefits of conducting business with you.

Jesus did.

That is why He was a Double-Diamond.

JESUS OVERCAME THE STIGMA OF A QUESTIONABLE BACKGROUND.

Your past is over.

Are you having self-doubts today? This is common. Your limited education. Your father dying when you were young. An alcoholic parent. Guilt over a serious mistake you made in your teenage years. It is very important that you remember your past is over.

Never build your future around your past.

Jesus was born with a terrible stigma. His mother Mary, was pregnant with Him before she ever married Joseph, His father. The Bible says that they had not had a sexual relationship, but, "that which is conceived in her is of the Holy Ghost." *(Matthew 1:20)*

Only two people in the world really knew that Mary was a virgin: God and Mary.

Undoubtedly, hundreds of people mocked and sneered at Joseph for marrying Mary.

Jesus grew up with this. He stepped out of a cesspool of human scorn. He clawed His way out of a pit of questions. He ignored the slanderous remarks. He knew the truth. He knew who He was and what He was about. It did not matter that others did not believe. *He chose to chart His own course.* The opinions of others did not matter.

God Never Consults Your Past
To Determine Your Future.

He never looked back. He never discussed the situation with anyone. There is not a single scripture in the entire Bible where He ever brought up His background or His limitations.

You too, can move beyond the scars of yesterday. Stop talking about your limited education. Quit complaining that everyone in your family is poor. Stop repeating stories of those who failed you. Stop pointing your finger at the economy.

Stop advertising your pain. Stop meditating on your flaws. Everyone has limitations. Each of us are handicapped in some way. Physically. Emotionally. Mentally. Spiritually.

Stop Looking At Where You Have Been And
Start Looking At Where You Are Going.

Concentrate on your *future.*
Jesus did.
That is what made Him a Double-Diamond.

JESUS NEVER WASTED TIME ANSWERING CRITICS.

Critics are spectators, not players.

Critical people are usually disheartened people who have failed to reach a desired goal. Someone has said, "Criticism is the death gargle of a non-achiever."

There has never been a monument built to a critic.

Critical people are *disappointed* people. *Disillusioned* people. *Unfocused* people. They are hurting inside. They build their life trying to destroy others.

Move away from them.

Don't get me wrong, debate is a marvelous arena. Conflict unlocks my energy.

But there is a place to present facts. There is a time for exchange of information. Constructive suggestions are always pursued by champions.

But there is a time for *silence.*

When Jesus was being ridiculed, and prepared for His crucifixion, He was silent. "But Jesus held His peace." *(Matthew 26:63)* Jesus did not feel obligated to answer critics. He never wasted time on people who were obviously trying to trap Him. He responded to *hunger.* He responded to *thirst.* He responded to *reachers.*

Double-Diamond Principle

**Never Spend More Time On A Critic
Than You Would Give To A Friend.**

You owe nothing to a critic. "Speak not in the ears of a fool: for he will despise the wisdom of thy words." *(Proverbs 23:9)*

Criticism is deadly.

Correction is life.

Criticism is pointing out your flaws.

Correction is pointing out your potential.

Many years ago I sat down at my kitchen table to reply to a critical letter from a lady. I toiled over my reply. I erased words, and wrote new sentences. It took me over one hour of exhausting work to carefully carve out a decent reaction to her letter. I still wasn't satisfied with my answer to her. Suddenly I began to laugh as a thought dawned. It suddenly hit me that I had never spent an entire hour writing a letter to my own mother, the dearest person in the world to me. I had never spent one hour writing to the woman who had carried me within her womb for nine months...provided comfort and food during my life...motivated me toward God and to learn to play the piano. I had not spent that much time on the most important person in my life. I was a fool to spend that much time on a critic.

Jesus ignored the critics.

That is why He was a Double-Diamond.

JESUS KNEW THERE WAS A RIGHT TIME AND A WRONG TIME TO APPROACH PEOPLE.

There is a time for everything.
There is a right time to approach people.

Suppose you want a raise. You really want to discuss it with your boss and what you can do to be worth more to him. If you have just made a terrible mistake that has cost the company $15,000.00, that is not the right time to approach him about your raise. If the company has just experienced incredible profits because of an idea that you shared with your boss, that might be the proper climate and atmosphere to discuss it with him.

Jesus understood timing. He spent 30 years preparing for His ministry before He launched His first miracle. When His mother told Him that they had no wine at the wedding Jesus responded to her, "Mine hour is not yet come." *(John 2:4)*

There is a time to ask for forgiveness, there is a time to be silent. There is a time to make presentations to people. There is a time to wait.

People are in different seasons of their life. Moods change. Circumstances affect our decisions. *Be sensitive to this.*

Double-Diamond
Principle

Your Entry Can Decide How You Exit.

It is a rare husband who can anticipate the moods, and needs of his wife and react appropriately. It is a brilliant teenager who knows and understands proper timing in discussing problems with his parents.

Jesus understood timing. When they caught the woman in the act of adultery His reaction was unique. "And Jesus said unto her, Neither do I condemn thee: go, and sin no more." *(John 8:11)*

He did not ignore her sin. He did not ignore the accusatory tone of the men wanting to trap her. He simply knew there was a proper time to do things. He did not dissect the woman's sin. He did not unravel the details of the adulterous act. He never dwelled on the past, but pointed people toward their future. There was a time for that.

"To everything there is a season, and a time to every purpose under the heaven:" "He hath made everything beautiful in His time." *(Ecclesiastes 3:1,11)*

Your success depends on timing. Don't forget it. Whether you sell to a customer, or sit at the discussion table with your supervisor. Stay sensitive to others. Observe. Watch. Listen to the flow of information and what is going on.

Jesus did.

That is why He was a Double-Diamond.

JESUS EDUCATED HIS DOWN-LINE.

You will always remember what you teach.

Someone has said that you don't learn anything when you talk. You only learn when you listen. That is inaccurate. Some of my greatest thoughts and ideas have surfaced while I was teaching others.

It is very important that you mentor someone. Train them. Teach them what you know. Especially your down-line. (Remember your down-line is any person who is carrying out an instruction for you, employees, children, or whoever.)

Successful businesses have employees who are informed, well trained and confident about carrying out their instructions. This takes time. It takes energy. It takes great patience.

It is a master secret in becoming a Double-Diamond in life.

Every song needs a singer. Every achiever needs motivation. Every student needs a teacher.

Jesus was a master teacher. He taught thousands at a time. Sometimes, He sat with His twelve disciples and fed information into them. He kept them motivated, influenced and inspired.

He taught them about prayer. *(Matthew 26:36-46)* He taught them about heaven. *(John 14:2-4)* He taught them about hell. *(Luke 16:20-31)* He educated His staff on many topics including His death, giving, and relationships.

Double-Diamond Principle

**You Will Always Remember
What You Teach.**

Jesus taught in synagogues. *(Luke 13:10)* He also taught in the villages. *(Mark 6:6)*

Here is the point. None of us were born with great knowledge. You become what you are. You *discovered* what you know. It took time, energy, and learning.

Your staff will not know everything. They may not see what you see. They may not feel what you feel. They may not have discovered what you know.

You must invest time to nurture their vision, their product knowledge and the rewards you want them to pursue.

You need good people around you. You need *inspired* people around you. You need *informed* people around you. You may be their *only* source for information and motivation.

Jesus educated His staff. Jesus constantly motivated His down-line by showing them the future of their present commitment.

Take the time to train others.

Jesus did.

That is why He was a Double-Diamond.

JESUS REFUSED TO BE DISCOURAGED WHEN OTHERS MISJUDGED HIS MOTIVES.

Everyone has been misjudged.

When a minister speaks on prosperity, he risks being accused of greed. When he prays for the sick, he risks being called a fraud and a fake.

Your own family may misjudge your motives. Your down-line may misjudge your actions.

Your boss might misread you. Customers may doubt your sincerity.

Don't be discouraged by that. Take the time to discuss your position with those who appear genuinely sincere. Do not waste your time and energy on those who are merely stirring up conflict.

Jesus was constantly misjudged by others. Pharisees accused Him of even being possessed by evil spirits. "But when the Pharisees heard it, they said, This fellow doth not cast out devils, but by Beelzebub the prince of devils." *(Matthew 12:24)* Let me make a few suggestions. When you speak to others, be concise. Be bold but very distinct in what you say. Do not leave room for misunderstandings when possible.

Double-Diamond
Principle

**False Accusation Is The Last Stage
Before Supernatural Promotion.**

Let me make a few suggestions.

Always be where you are. When you are in conversation with someone, totally focus on that conversation. Shut out everything else. When you totally focus on what you are saying and hearing, you do not have to reflect later on with regret about that conversation. This can prevent unnecessary misjudgment.

Every extraordinary achiever has been misjudged. People laughed over the thought of a horseless carriage. Others sneered when the telephone was invented.

Your success is on the other side of scorn and false accusations.

Jesus knew this.

That is why He was a Double-Diamond.

JESUS REFUSED TO BE BITTER WHEN OTHERS WERE DISLOYAL OR BETRAYED HIM.

Bitterness is more devastating than betrayal.

Betrayal is external. Bitterness is internal. You see, betrayal is something that *others do to you*. Bitterness is something you do to yourself.

Thousands survive the currents of bitterness. "Looking diligently lest any man fail of the grace of God; lest any root of bitterness springing up trouble you, and thereby many be defiled." *(Hebrews 12:15)*

Disloyalty is a product of an unthankful heart. Betrayal is usually the child of jealousy.

Everybody has experienced these tragic situations in their life. An unfaithful mate, an employee who slanders you behind your back. A boss who fires you without explanation. These things hurt. Deeply.

Jesus was at supper with His disciples. "And as they sat and did eat, Jesus said, Verily I say unto you, One of you which eateth with me shall betray me." *(Mark 14:18)* Jesus knew *who* would betray Him. He knew *how* he would betray Him. He knew *when* He would be betrayed. Yet, He saw something *more important* than the hurt and wounds of betrayal.

Double-Diamond Principle

Injustice Is Only As Powerful As Your Memory Of It.

Read Mark 14:43-50 and you will see one of the most demoralizing experiences any human can experience. Judas betrayed Him with a kiss.

Yet Jesus refused to be bitter.

Neither did He penalize Judas. Judas destroyed himself. He did not disconnect from Peter who denied Him. Peter cried out for mercy and forgiveness. He was restored and became the great preacher on the Day Of Pentecost.

"Let all bitterness, and wrath, and anger, and clamor, and evil speaking, be put away from you, with all malice: and be ye kind one to another, tender-hearted, forgiving one another, even as God for Christ sake hath forgiven you." *(Ephesians 4:31-32)*

Eliminate any words of bitterness in every conversation. Do not remind others of your experience unless it is to teach and encourage them to rise above their own hurts.

Jesus saw the chapter beyond betrayal.

He refused to be bitter.

That is why He became a Double-Diamond.

JESUS NETWORKED WITH PEOPLE OF ALL BACKGROUNDS.

Greatness is everywhere.

People have different contributions. I believe you need different kinds of input into your life. Someone needs what you possess. You need something that they can contribute to you. You are the sum total of your experiences.

Personalities differ. Each person around you contains a different body of knowledge. It is up to you to "drop your pail in their well," and draw it out. "Where no counsel is, the people fall: but in the multitude of counsellors there is safety." *(Proverbs 11:14)*

Look at those who surrounded Jesus. A tax collector. A physician. Fishermen. A woman who had been possessed with seven devils.

Some were poor. Some were wealthy. Some were very energetic while others were passive. Some were explosive like Peter. Others, like James, were logical.

Be willing to listen to others. Everyone sees through different eyes. They feel with different hearts. They hear through different ears. *Someone knows something that you should know.* You will not discover it until you take the time to stop and hear them out. *One piece of information can turn a failure into a success.* Great decisions are products of great thought.

Double-Diamond Principle

Diamonds Will Pay Any Price To Stay In The Presence Of Extraordinary People.

Jesus networked.
That is why He was a Double-Diamond.

JESUS RESISTED TEMPTATION.

Everybody is tempted.

Temptation is the presentation of evil. It is an opportunity to choose temporary pleasure rather than permanent gain.

You will experience many seasons during your life. During your teenage years, you may feel overwhelming currents of lust toward immorality. In your business world, you will be tempted to distort the truth, cheat on your taxes or even "pocket extra money for yourself." Unfaithful mates are epidemic. Billboards boldly declare their invitation to alcohol. Drugs are on every corner. Cocaine appears to be an escape, to many, from the complexities of life.

Satan is a master artist.

Jesus experienced a relentless and persistent adversary, the devil. It happened after He had fasted forty days and forty nights. His defense was quite simple: the written WORD OF GOD. "Then was Jesus led up of the Spirit into the wilderness to be tempted of the devil. And when the tempter came to Him, he said, If thou be the Son of God, command that these stones be made bread. But He answered and said, It is written, Man shall not live by bread alone, but by every word that proceedeth out of the mouth of God. Then the devil taketh Him up into the holy city, and setteth Him on a pinnacle of the temple, And saith unto Him, If thou be the Son of God, cast thyself down: for it is written, He shall give His angels charge concerning thee: and in their hands they shall bear thee up, lest at any time thou dash thy foot against a stone. Jesus said unto him, It is written again, Thou shalt not tempt the Lord thy God. Again, the devil taketh Him up into an exceeding high mountain, and sheweth Him all the kingdoms of the world, and the glory of them; And saith unto Him, All these things will I give thee, if thou wilt fall down and worship me. Then saith Jesus unto him, Get thee hence, Satan: for it is written, Thou shalt worship the Lord thy God, and Him only shalt thou serve. Then the devil leaveth Him, and, behold, angels came and ministered unto Him." *(Matthew 4:1-11)*

**One Night Of Pleasure Is Not Worth A
Lifetime Of Blindness.**

The graveyard is full of people who failed to resist satan. The prisons are overcrowded with people too weak to stand against him. Dreams crash daily on the rocks of temptation.

Move the ship of your life away from those rocks. Ask Samson and he will tell you, "One night of pleasure is not worth a lifetime of blindness."

Fight Back.

Jesus did.

That is why He was a Double-Diamond.

JESUS MADE DECISIONS THAT CREATED A DESIRED FUTURE INSTEAD OF A DESIRED PRESENT.

Decisions create events.

If you eat two slices of pecan pie every night, what is the inevitable eventuality? If you smoke two packs of cigarettes daily, what is the inevitable eventuality? Everything you are presently doing will benefit your *present*...or your *future*. The choice is yours.

You will make a lot of decisions today. Some of them will pleasure you...today. But tomorrow you will be miserable over those decisions. Some of those decisions may make you a little uncomfortable for today. But, tomorrow, you will be thrilled.

Tonight you will sit down at supper. Your mouth will water at the beautiful chocolate cake someone has prepared. You will make a decision about that chocolate cake. If you eat it, it will taste good...for now. Tomorrow morning you will feel it and be unhappy with yourself for not refusing it. If you look at that piece of cake and say, "I'm going to make a decision that *benefits my future.* I refuse it." That is the decision of a champion.

Double-Diamond Principle

Diamonds Make Decisions That Will Create The Future They Desire.

Jesus could have called ten thousand angels to deliver Him from the crucifixion. He was capable of coming down off of the cross. But, He made the decision in the garden of Gethsemane that created an incredible future. *He was willing to go through a season of pain to create an eternity of gain.*

"For our light affliction, which is but for a moment, worketh for us a far more exceeding and eternal weight of glory." *(II Corinthians 4:17)*

Those who can wait...usually win. Those who refuse to wait...usually lose. Patience is powerful. It is productive.

Reprogram your thinking to distance. Reprogram your life for endurance. Start thinking "long term" about your eating habits. Your prayer life. Your friendships.

Jesus was a "long termer."

That is why He was a Double-Diamond.

JESUS NEVER JUDGED PEOPLE BY THEIR OUTWARD APPEARANCE.

Nobody is ever as they first appear.

Packaging is deceptive. Cereal boxes make drab cereal look like the most exciting food in the world. Billions of dollars are spent on packaging.

Don't get me wrong. Clothing is very important. Appearance sells or discourages. Proverbs 7 talks about the clothing of a prostitute. Proverbs 31 describes the clothes of a virtuous woman. Most assuredly, *it is wise to create a climate of acceptance.* Naomi, the mentor of Ruth, instructed her to put on perfume and change her clothes before she went to meet Boaz, her future husband.

But, something is more important than the packaging. *The person.*

Jesus saw a scarred and weary woman who had been married five times. He saw beyond her failures and reputation. He saw her *heart.* He saw a *desire to be changed.* She was the golden bridge for Jesus to walk into the hearts of many of those people of her city. "And many of the Samaritans of that city believed on Him for the saying of the woman, which testified, He told me all that ever I did." *(John 4:39)*

Double-Diamond Principle

Nothing Is Ever As It First Appears.

People saw Zaccheus as a conniving, deceptive tax collector. Jesus saw a confused man who longed for a change of heart. People of Israel saw in Absalom a handsome, articulate leader. He was a traitor and liar. Samson thought Delilah was the most beautiful woman he had ever met. She was the trap that destroyed his championship status.

An interesting story was shared recently by a friend of mine in Florida. She owns a clothing store. She said, "I have had ladies come to my store who looked like they did not have a penny to their name. Yet, purchase thousands of dollars worth of clothing, get into their chauffeured limousine and drive off. You could not tell what they possessed by what they wore."

Nothing is ever as it first appears.

Start listening for attitudes in people. Start listening for hurts. Don't misjudge them.

Jesus knew this.

That is why He was a Double-Diamond.

JESUS RECOGNIZED THE LAW OF REPETITION.

What you hear repeatedly, you eventually will believe.

Teachers know that the basic law of learning is *repetition.* Someone has said you must hear something sixteen times before you really believe it.

Notice the television commercials. You have seen the same ones repeatedly. Billboards advertise well-known soft drinks...over and over again. Why? You must *keep hearing* something, seeing something, before you respond to it.

It simply takes *time* to absorb a message.

Jesus taught people the same truths again and again. *"Then spake Jesus AGAIN unto them."* (John 8:12)

Someone taught you everything you know today. You are the result of a process. There was a time in your life that you could not even spell the word "cat." You did not know numbers. But somebody was patient with you.

Great achievers understand the necessity of teaching those around them...*again and again.*

Double-Diamond Principle

**What You Hear Repeatedly,
You Will Eventually Believe.**

Don't expect your down-line (those who are networked with you) to understand everything instantly. You did not. They will not either. It takes time to grow greatness.

Jesus knew this.

That is why He was a Double-Diamond.

JESUS WAS A TOMORROW THINKER.

Become a "tomorrow thinker."

One of the great companies in Japan has a detailed plan for the next 100 years. They are *tomorrow thinkers.*

Jesus was a tomorrow thinker. When He met the Samaritan woman at the well, He barely mentioned that she had been married five times. *He pointed her to her future.* He said that He would give her water and she would never thirst again.

Another remarkable illustration of tomorrow thinking concerns the woman caught in the act of adultery. He never discussed her sin. He simply said unto her, "Neither do I condemn thee: go, and sin no more." *(John 8:11)*

"Remember ye not the former things, neither consider the things of old. Behold, I will do a new thing; now it shall spring forth; shall ye not know it? I will even make a way in the wilderness, and rivers in the desert." *(Isaiah 43:18, 19)*

Double-Diamond Principle

**Those Who Created Yesterday's Pain
Do Not Control Tomorrow's Potential.**

Satan discusses your past. That appears to be the only information he has. Jesus discusses your *future.* He enters your life to end your past and give birth to tomorrow.

Stop taking journeys into yesterday.

Jesus concentrated on the future.

That is why He was a Double-Diamond.

JESUS KNEW THAT MONEY ALONE COULD NOT BRING CONTENTMENT.

Rich people are not always happy people.

Your hands can be full of money. Your head can be full of information. But if your heart is empty, your life is very empty.

Money is for movement, not accumulation. That is why the Bible talks about "the deceitfulness of riches."

Jesus saw this. He talked to the rich. He looked into their eyes and saw a longing for *something that money could not buy.* They came to Him late at night, when the crowds were gone. They were lonely. "For a man's life consisteth not in the abundance of the things which he possesseth." *(Luke 12:15)*

Solomon was a wealthy king. Yet he confessed, "Therefore I hated life;" *(Ecclesiastes 2:17)*

Prosperity Is Having Enough Of God's Provision To Complete His Purpose For Your Life.

Think for a moment. You probably possess more today than any time in your whole life. Do you feel more joy than you've ever had in your life? Do you laugh more now than you've ever laughed? Do you enjoy your friendships more than you ever have? Be honest with yourself.

Jesus knew "The eyes of man are never satisfied." *(Proverbs 27:20) Some things matter more than money.*

Jesus knew this.
That is why He was a Double-Diamond.

JESUS KNEW THE POWER OF WORDS AND THE POWER OF SILENCE.

Words are not cheap.

Wars begin because of *words*. Peace comes when great men get together and negotiate and dialogue. *Words link people.* Words are the bridge into your future.

Words *created the world. (Genesis 1:3-31)*

Words *create your world. (Proverbs 18:21)*

Jesus said that your words reveal what kind of heart you possess. "For of the abundance of the heart his mouth speaketh." *(Luke 6:45)*

Jesus said words can move mountains. (Mark 11:23)

There is a time to *talk*. There is a time to *listen*. There is a time for *movement*. There is a time for *staying still*. When people were hungry for knowledge, Jesus spoke and taught for hours. But, when He got to Pontius Pilate's hall where truth was ignored, He was silent.

Your *words* matter. Conversation matters. "But I say unto you, that every idle word that men shall speak, they shall give account thereof in the day of judgement. For by thy words thou shalt be justified, and by thy words thou shalt be condemned." *(Matthew 12:36-37)* Be silent...about injustices to you. Be silent...in discussing the weaknesses of others. Be silent... in advertising your own mistakes.

Double-Diamond
Principle

Silence Cannot Be Misquoted.

Jesus knew when to talk... and when to listen.
That is why He was a Double-Diamond.

JESUS KNEW WHEN YOU WANTED SOMETHING YOU HAVE NEVER HAD, YOU HAVE GOT TO DO SOMETHING YOU HAVE NEVER DONE.

Everything is difficult at first.

When you were beginning to crawl, it was very difficult. When you took your first step, and fell...that was difficult.

Thousands will fail in life because they are unwilling to make changes. They refuse to change jobs, towns, or friendships. They stay in comfort zones. Yet, thousands of others move up the ladder of happiness because they are willing to go through a little discomfort to experience a new level in life.

Peter wanted to walk on water. Jesus saw his excitement. Then He gave a simple instruction for Peter to do something he had never done before. And He said, "come." "And when Peter was come down out of the ship he walked on the water, to go to Jesus." *(Matthew 14:28-29)*

Jesus always gave people something to do. And it was always something *they had never done before.* He knew that their obedience was the only proof of their faith in Him.

Listen to the instructions to the Israelites: march around the walls of Jericho seven days in a row, and then seven times on Sunday.

Double-Diamond Principle

**When You Want Something
You Have Never Had,
You Have Got To Do Something
You Have Never Done.**

Listen to the prophets instructions to a leper: go dip in the Jordan river seven times. You will be healed on the seventh time.

Ruth left her home country of Moab to be with Naomi, she met Boaz who changed her life forever.

Elijah stretched the faith of the widow who was down to her last meal. Two pancakes before death, he motivated her to do something she had never done--sow her seed in expectation of a harvest during famine. She saw the miracle come to pass.

Jesus knew how to stretch people's faith. He motivated them. *He helped them do things they had never done before in order to create things they had never had.*

Jesus did new things.

That is why He was a Double-Diamond.

JESUS PERMITTED OTHERS TO CORRECT THEIR MISTAKES.

Everybody makes mistakes. Everybody.

Examine the biographies of multimillionaires. Many have experienced bankruptcy several times. They simply discovered that failure is not fatal. *Failure is merely an opinion.*

Jesus never disconnected from those who made mistakes with their life.

One of His favorite disciples was Peter. Peter denied Him. Yet, he confessed his sin. Jesus forgave him. He became one of the greatest apostles in the history of the church.

David committed adultery with Bathsheba. God forgave him. Look at Samson. He fell into sexual temptation with Delilah. Yet, he is one of the champions of faith mentioned in Hebrews 11:32.

Learn to forgive *yourself.* Learn to forgive *others.* Everybody hurts somewhere. Their mistakes stay on their mind. *Give them another chance.*

Double-Diamond Principle

All Men Fall.
The Great Ones Get Back Up.

Mistakes are correctable.
Jesus knew this.
That is why He was a Double-Diamond.

JESUS KNEW HIS WORTH.

Know your gift.

Many around you may never discover you. It is not really important that they do. *What is really important is that you discover yourself, your gifts, your talents.*

Popularity is when *other people* like you. Happiness is *when you like yourself.*

There is an interesting scenario when Jesus visited the home of Lazarus and his two sisters, Mary and Martha. Martha, busy with housework, was agitated with Mary who was simply sitting at the feet of Jesus listening to every word He said. When she complained, Jesus replied, "Mary hath chosen that good part." *(Luke 10:38-42)*

He knew His personal worth. He knew that His own words were life. He was incredibly self-confident and *expected to be treated well.*

He honored those who discerned His worth.

Jesus even reacted favorably to a woman who washed His feet. "Seest thou this woman? I entered into thine house, thou gavest me no water for my feet: but she hath washed my feet with tears, and wiped them with hairs of her head. Thou gavest me no kiss: but this woman since the time I came in, hath not ceased to kiss my feet. My head with oil thou didst not anoint: but this woman hath anointed my feet with ointment." *(Luke 7:44-46)*

Double-Diamond Principle

Happiness Is When You Like Yourself.

Jesus knew His worth.
That is why He was a Double-Diamond.

JESUS NEVER TRIED TO SUCCEED ALONE.

You need people.

You need God.

Everything you have came from God. Success is a collection of relationships. Without clients, a lawyer has no career. Without patients, a doctor has no future. Without a composer, a singer has nothing to say.

Your future is connected to people, so develop people skills.

Jesus knew the importance of others.

He constantly talked to His *Up-line* (His Heavenly Father.) He talked to His *Down-line* (His disciples.) He talked to everybody. At twelve, He exchanged with the scribes and priests in the temple. He talked to tax collectors, fishermen, doctors, and lawyers. He said, "I can of mine self do nothing." *(John 5:30)*

You need problem-solvers in your life.

You need a good banker, doctor, and a financial advisor. You need your family. You need a Godly pastor. You need people.

Double-Diamond
Principle

**Your Rewards In Life Are Determined By
The Problems You Solve For Someone Else.**

Listen to the inner voice of the Holy Spirit today. Obey every instruction.

Jesus did.

That is why He was a Double-Diamond.

JESUS KNEW THAT MONEY IS ANYWHERE YOU REALLY WANT IT TO BE.

Money is everywhere.

Money is anything of value. Your *time* is money. Your *knowledge* is money. Your *skills, gifts* and *talents* are money.

Stop seeing money as merely something you carry around in your wallet. View money as *anything you possess that solves a problem for someone.*

Money is everywhere. Jesus knew that money even existed in the most unlikely places. Money is *anywhere* you really want it to be.

Colonel Sanders wanted it to be in *something he loved*, his unique fried chicken. Mohammed Ali found his financial success in boxing.

Peter was a fisherman. Tax money was needed. Jesus told him where money could be found. "Lest we should offend them, go thou to the sea, and cast an hook, and take up the fish that first cometh up; and when thou hast opened his mouth, thou shalt find a piece of money: that take, and give unto them for me and thee." *(Matthew 17:27)*

Double-Diamond Principle

**Money Exists in The Most Unlikely Places.
Look.**

Do you love flowers and long to make your living owning a florist shop? That is where your money can be found.

Jesus knew that money existed *everywhere*.

That is why He was a Double-Diamond.

JESUS SET SPECIFIC GOALS.

Decide what you really want.

In 1952 a prominent university discovered that only three out of one hundred graduates had written down a clear list of goals. Ten years later, their follow up study showed that three percent of the graduating class had accomplished more financially than the remaining ninety-seven percent of the class.

Those three percent were the *same graduates* who had *written down their goals.* "Write the vision, and make it plain upon tables, that he may run that readeth it." *(Habakkuk 2:2)*

When you decide exactly *"what"* you want, the *"how to do it"* will emerge.

Jesus knew His purpose and mission. "For the son of man has come to seek and to save that which is lost." *(Luke 19:10)*

He knew the product He had to offer. "The thief cometh not, but for to steal, and to kill, and to destroy: I have come that they might have life, and they might have it more abundantly." *(John 10:10)*

Jesus had a sense of destiny. He knew where He wanted to go. He knew where people needed Him. *(John 4:3)*

Double-Diamond Principle

When You Decide What You Want, The "How-To-Do-It" Will Emerge.

Jesus knew that achievers were detail oriented. "For which of you, intending to build a tower, sitteth not down first, and counteth the cost, whether you have sufficient to finish it?" *(Luke 14:28)*

Take four sheets of paper. At the top of sheet number one, write, "My lifetime dreams and goals."

Now write in total detail everything you would like to become, do, or have during your lifetime. *Dream your dreams in detail on paper.*

Now, take sheet number two and write, "My twelve month goals."

Now list everything you want to get done within the next twelve months.

Now, take the third sheet of paper and write, "My thirty day goals."

Now write out in detail what you would like to accomplish for the next thirty days.

Now take the fourth sheet of paper and write, "My ideal success daily routine."

Now write down the seven most important things you will do in the next twenty-four hours.

The secret of your future is hidden in your daily routine. Set your goals.

Jesus knew this.

That is why He was a Double-Diamond.

JESUS KNEW THAT EVERY GREAT ACHIEVEMENT REQUIRED A WILLINGNESS TO BEGIN SMALL.

Everything big starts little.

Think for just a moment. An oak tree began as an acorn. A six foot man began as a small, small embryo in a mother's womb.

Be willing to begin small. *Start with whatever you have.* Everything you possess is a starting point. Do not be like the man in the Bible who had one talent and refused to use it. *Use whatever you have been given, and more will come to you.*

Jesus began in a stable. But He did not stay there. He went thirty years without performing miracles. But one day He launched His first miracle. The rest is history.

David had a slingshot. But he *became* a king.

Joseph was sold as a slave. But he *became* the Prime Minister of Egypt.

The widow of Zarephath had a small pancake. But she sowed it into the work of God and created a continuous supply during the famine.

Whatever you have been given is enough to create anything you have been promised.

Double-Diamond Principle

Whatever You Have In Your Hand Can Create Anything You Want In Your Future.

"For who hath despised the day of small things." *(Zechariah 4:10)* "For precept must be on precept, precept on precept; line upon line, line upon line; here a little, and there a little." *(Isaiah 28:10)*

Whatever you possess today is enough to create anything else you will ever want in your future.

Jesus existed before the foundation of the world. He remembered when the earth and the human race did not even exist. That is why He did not mind the beginning in a stable.

Jesus knew *great things started small.*

That is why He was a Double-Diamond.

JESUS HURT WHEN OTHERS HURT.

Someone close to you is in trouble.

Have you really noticed it? Does it matter to you at all? Everybody hurts somewhere. When others hurt, try to feel it.

You are a solution to somebody with a problem. Find them. Listen for their cry.

You are their walking life jacket. You hold the key to their lock. Feel it.

Jesus did. Jesus did not hide in the palace. He was not a recluse. He walked where people walked. He hurt when people hurt.

"And Jesus went forth, and saw a great multitude, and was moved with compassion toward them, and He healed their sick." (Matthew 14:14)

Jesus feels what you feel. "For we have not an high priest which cannot be touched with the feeling of our infirmities; but was in all points tempted like as we are, yet without sin." (Hebrews 4:15)

You will begin to succeed with your life when the hurt and problems of others begin to matter to you.

Double-Diamond Principle

The Broken Become Masters At Mending.

Several years ago, I was invited to attend a Christmas party for a large law firm here in Dallas. One of the young lawyers told an unforgettable story that night. He was the protégé of one of the great lawyers in the midwest. This renowned lawyer won practically every case. In fact, every one of his settlements were million dollar settlements. The young lawyer simply could not figure it out. He said, "The research was normal. The reading material seemed normal. The stack of information we had collected seemed average before he got in front of the jury."

Then he said, "This old lawyer could walk back and forth before the jury. As he talked, a transformation took place on the faces of the jury. When they came back they always gave his client huge settlements."

That night at the Christmas party, the young lawyer told us how he probed his mentor and said, "You must tell me your secret. I watch you carefully. I've read your material. But, none of us in the firm can figure out why your juries returned with million dollar verdicts. It is a mystery we cannot unravel."

The old lawyer said, "I would like to tell you, but you really would not believe me if I did."

The young lawyer probed him month after month. For a long time the older lawyer insisted, "It really would not mean anything to you."

Finally one day when the young protégé was going to leave his firm to another city, the old mentor said, "Take a drive with me." They went to a grocery store. The old lawyer filled the back of his car with groceries and they began to drive out into the country. It had snowed. It was freezing and the icy weather was cutting. They finally drove up to a very modest, inexpensive farm house. The old mentor instructed the young lawyer to help him carry in the groceries. When they went inside the home, the young lawyer saw a little boy sitting on a sofa. He looked closer and noticed that the little boy had both of his legs cut off. It happened in a car accident. The old lawyer spoke to the family for a few moments and said, "Just thought I would bring a few groceries for you since I know how difficult it is for you to get out in this kind of weather."

As they were driving back to the city, the old lawyer looked at the young lawyer and said, "It is quite simple. My clients *really do matter to me.* I *believe* in their cases. I *believe* they deserve the highest settlements that can be given. When I stand before a jury, somehow *they feel that.* They come back with the verdicts I desire. *I feel what my clients feel.* The jury *feels* what I *feel.*"

Double-Diamond
Principle

**Those Who Unlock Your Compassion Are
Those To Whom You Have Been Assigned.**

Jesus hurts when others hurt.
That is why He was a Double-Diamond.

JESUS WAS NOT AFRAID TO SHOW HIS FEELINGS.

Emotions dictate world events.

An angered world leader attacks another country. Angry airline employees have a picket line at airports. A mother whose child is killed by a drunk driver launches a national campaign. Thousands are rallying to stop the abortions of millions of babies.

Feelings do matter in life.

In business, feelings are contagious. When a salesman is excited over his product, the customer feels it, and is influenced by it.

Jesus was not afraid to express Himself.

When He was infuriated, others knew it. "And the Jews' Passover was at hand, and Jesus went up to Jerusalem, And found in the temple those that sold oxen and sheep and doves...And when he had made a scourge of small cords, he drove them all out of the temple, and the sheep, and the oxen: and poured out the changers' money, and overthrew the tables." *(John 2:13-15)*

He was deeply moved with compassion when He saw multitudes wandering aimlessly without direction. "But when he saw the multitudes, he was moved with compassion on them, because they were faint, and were scattered abroad, as sheep having no shepherd." *(Matthew 9:36)*

Double-Diamond Principle

The Problem That Infuriates You The Most, Is The Problem God Has Assigned You To Solve.

The Bible even records that Jesus wept openly. "And when he was come near, he beheld the city, and wept over it." *(Luke 19:41)*

I am not speaking about an uncontrollable temper, neither am I referring to someone who sobs and breaks down every time a problem occurs in their life.

Rather, I'm asking that you notice that Jesus did not bottle up His emotions. He was not a robot. He was enthusiastic when He saw a demonstration of faith, He wept when He saw unbelief.

Peter, His disciple, was affected by it. The Apostle Paul was set on fire by it. They changed the course of history.

Be bold in expressing your opinions. Feel strongly about the things that matter in life. You can be a marvelous influence for good.

You will always be drawn to people who are expressive. Thousands scream at rock concerts, football games and world championship boxing matches.

Don't be a spectator of life. *Get in the arena.*

Jesus was.

That is why He was a Double-Diamond.

JESUS KNEW THE POWER OF HABIT.

Great men simply have great habits.

A well known billionaire said, "I arrive at my office at 7:00 a.m. It is a habit." Recently a best selling novelist who has sold over one million books said, "I get up at the same time every morning. I start writing at 8:00 a.m. And I quit at 4:00 each afternoon. I do it every day. It is a habit."

Habit is a gift from God. *It simply means anything you do twice becomes easier.* It is the Creator's key in helping you succeed.

Jesus stayed busy. He traveled. He prayed for the sick. He taught and ministered. He supervised His disciples. He spoke to large crowds.

However, He had an important custom and habit. "And he came to Nazareth, where he had been brought up: AND AS HIS CUSTOM WAS, he went into the synagogue on the sabbath day, and stood up for to read." *(Luke 4:16)*

Double-Diamond
Principle

You Will Never Change Your Life Until You Change Something You Do Daily.

Daniel prayed three times a day. *(Daniel 6:10)* The psalmist prayed seven times daily. *(Psalms 119:164)* The disciples of Jesus met on the first day of each week. *(Acts 20:7)*

Jesus knew *great men simply have great habits.*

That is why He was a Double-Diamond.

JESUS FINISHED WHAT HE STARTED.

Champions are finishers.

It is fun to be creative. It is exciting to always be giving birth to new ideas, thinking of new places to go or launching a new product. But real champions complete things. They are *follow through* people.

Jesus was thirty years old when He started His ministry. His ministry went for three and half years. He did many miracles. He touched many lives. He electrified the world through twelve men.

But hidden in the thousands of scriptures is a golden principle that revealed His power. It happened on the horrible day of His crucifixion. He was taunted by thousands. Spears pierced His side. Spikes were driven into His hands. Eight inches of thorns were crushed into His brow. Blood had dried on His hair. Four hundred soldiers left spittle running down His body.

That is when He uttered perhaps the greatest sentence ever uttered on earth: "It is finished." *(John 19:30)* The sins of man could be forgiven. He paid the price. The plan was complete. He was the lamb led to the slaughter.

He was the chief cornerstone. *(Ephesians 2:20) The Prince of Peace had come. (Isaiah 9:6)* Our great high priest, the Son of God, was our golden link to the God of heaven. *(Hebrews 4:14)*

Double-Diamond
Principle

Your Exit Will Be Remembered Longer Than Your Entry.

Jesus was a finisher. He finished what He started. The bridge that linked man to God was complete. Man could approach God without fear.

The Apostle Paul was a finisher. *(II Timothy 4:7)*

Solomon, the wisest man that ever lived was a finisher. *(I Kings 6:14)*

One famous multi-millionaire said, "I will pay a great salary to anyone who can complete an instruction that I give to him."

Start completing *little things.* Write that "Thank you" note to your friend. Make those two telephone calls.

Get the spirit of a finisher. "He that endureth to the end shall be saved." *(Matthew 10:22)*

Jesus was a Finisher.

That is why He was a Double-Diamond.

JESUS WAS KNOWLEDGEABLE OF SCRIPTURE.

When God talks, the wise listen.

The greatest book on earth is the Bible. It has outsold every book. It is the Word of God.

It takes approximately 56 hours to read the Bible through completely. If you read 40 chapters a day, you will complete the Bible within 30 days. If you read nine chapters a day in the New Testament, you will finish reading the New Testament within 30 days. You should read the Bible systematically. Regularly. Expectantly.

Read Luke 4. When satan presented his temptation to Christ, Jesus merely quoted scriptures back to him as answers. *The Word of God is powerful.* "Thy word have I hid in mine heart, that I might not sin against thee." *(Psalms 119:11)*

The book of Proverbs has 31 chapters. Why not sit down today and start a magnificent new habit: reading this wisdom book completely through each month? Simply read chapter one on the first day of each month...chapter two on the second and so forth.

Double-Diamond Principle

Faith Comes When You Hear God Talk.

The Word of God will build your faith. "So then faith cometh by hearing, and hearing by the Word of God." *(Romans 10:17)* Faith comes when you *hear* God talk. Faith comes when you *speak* the Word of God.

The Word of God keeps you pure. "Wherewithal shall a young man cleanse his way? by taking heed thereto according to thy word." *(Psalms 119:9)*

Jesus knew the word.

That is why He was a Double-Diamond.

JESUS NEVER HURRIED.

Impatience is costly.

This is an impatient generation. Fast foods, microwave ovens, and crowded freeways reflect this philosophy.

Your greatest mistakes will happen because of impatience.

Most businesses that fail, do so because of lack of preparation and time. Great businesses do not happen overnight. Even this great country took years to become an independent nation.

Take time to grow into your business. Be deliberate with your projects. Become a "long-termer."

Life is a marathon, not a fifty-yard dash.

Champions pace themselves. They see the big picture.

Jesus refused to be rushed by the emergencies of others. There are no scriptures recorded that show where He was hurried or ever in an emergency.

When one of His close friends Lazarus was sick, word was sent to Jesus. Mary and Martha, the sisters of Lazarus, wanted Jesus TO HURRY and pray for his healing before he died. *Jesus kept His own agenda.* An unhurried and unrushed agenda. Lazarus died. Here is the story. "Now a certain man was sick, named Lazarus, of Bethany, the town of Mary and her sister, Martha, whose brother Lazarus was sick. Therefore, his sisters sent unto Him, saying, Lord, behold, he whom thou lovest is sick. When Jesus heard that, He said, This sickness is not unto death, but for the glory of God...Now Jesus loved Martha, and her sister, and Lazarus. When He had heard, therefore, He abode two days still in the same place where He was. Then said Martha unto Jesus, Lord, if thou hadst been here, my brother had not died...Jesus said unto her, Thy brother shall rise again...And when He thus had spoken, he cried with a loud voice, Lazarus, come forth. And he that was dead came forth, bound hand and foot with grave clothes; and his face was bound about with a cloth. Jesus saith unto them, Loose him, and let him go." *(John 11:1-44)*

Decisiveness is powerful and magnetic, but Jesus never made decisions due to pressure tactics from others. Refuse to be intimidated by statements such as, "This is the last one available this year. If you don't buy it now, you may not get another chance."

Double-Diamond
Principle

Patience is The Weapon That Forces Deception To Reveal Itself.

Skilled negotiators teach that *waiting is a weapon.* Whoever is the most hurried and impatient usually ends up with the worst end of the deal.

Take time to do things right. The weakness and flaws of any plan are often buried by flurry and hurry.

Jesus knew this.

That is why He was a Double-Diamond.

JESUS WENT WHERE HE WAS CELEBRATED INSTEAD OF WHERE HE WAS TOLERATED.

Never stay where you are not valued.

Never stay where you have not been assigned. Treasure your gift. Guard well any talent God has given to you. Know this--God has prepared those to receive you when you are at the place of your assignment.

Jesus was unable to do any miracles in certain cities. The people doubted. Unbelief was like a cancer in the atmosphere. It stopped Him from releasing the healing flow.

He taught His disciples to disconnect from any place that did not see their worth. "And whosoever shall not receive you, nor hear your words, when ye depart out of that house or city, shake off the dust of your feet." *(Matthew 10:14) (Proverbs 25:17)*

Double-Diamond Principle

Never Expect A 16x20 Idea To Be Celebrated By A 3x5 Mind.

It is foolish to waste your entire life on those who do not celebrate you. *Move on.*

Jesus did.

That is why He was a Double-Diamond.

JESUS CONSTANTLY CONSULTED HIS UP-LINE.

Learn to reach.

A famous billionaire of our day was trained by his father. In one of his recent books he said that he called his father a dozen time a week. He also telephones his own office ten to twelve times a day. He said, "If I don't constantly stay in touch with my business, it's gone." Stay in touch with your supervisor. Your boss. Regularly.

Remember, your Up-line is *anyone who supervises you, mentors you or is guiding you into something you want to accomplish.*

Jesus was brilliant. He was a miracle worker. He *constantly consulted* His heavenly father. "Then answered Jesus and said unto them, Verily, Verily, I say unto you, the Son can do nothing of himself, but what he seeth the Father do: for what things soever he doeth, these also doeth the Son likewise." *(John 5:19)*

Jesus was open to His Father about His feelings. In the garden of Gethsemane, He cried, "Oh my Father, if it be possible, let this cup pass from me: Nevertheless, not as I will, but as thou wilt." *(Matthew 26:39)*

Jesus was persistent in pursuing His father, His Up-line. "He went away again the second time, and prayed." *(Matthew 26:42,44)* Jesus felt alone. He lived in our world. He felt the feelings you feel. He is our elder brother. *And, He was not too proud to reach.*

Double-Diamond
Principle

Mentors Are Bridges To Tomorrow.

Diamonds know the power of connection. They *create* contact. They know it's the first step toward increase. *Somebody is a link to your future successes.* Tomorrow hinges on your ability to pursue them. Do it.

Jesus reached.

That is why He was a Double-Diamond.

JESUS KNEW THAT PRAYER GENERATED RESULTS.

Prayer works.

Satan dreads your prayer link to God. He will attempt to sabotage it in any way possible. Don't let him. *Make a daily appointment with God.* You make appointments with your dentist. You make appointments with your lawyer. Schedule a specific moment with God.

You will never be the same.

Jesus prayed during crisis times. Just before His crucifixion, He prayed three different times to His Father. *(Matthew 26:44)*

He taught His disciples how to pray. There are six important words to remember as you read "the Lord's Prayer." *(Matthew 6:6)*

1) *Praise.* "Our Father which art in heaven, Hallowed be thy name." *(Matthew 6:9)* Here is an important place to remember that God assigned Himself numerous names. Jehovah-Jirah which means "the Lord provideth." Jehovah-Raphe, "the Lord that heals."

2) *Priorities.* "Thy kingdom come. Thy will be done in earth, as it is in heaven." *(Matthew 6:10)* This is where you ask the Lord to implement His plan for each day. His will to be done in government, on your job, in your home, and in your personal life.

3) *Provision.* "Give us this day our daily bread." *(Matthew 6:11)* When you pray, begin to thank God that He is providing all the finances that you need for your life.

4) *Pardon.* "And forgive us our debts, as we forgive our debtors." *(Matthew 6:12)* Here, Jesus instructs His disciples to release forgiveness and pardon to those who have sinned against them. "What you make happen for others, God will make happen for you." Mercy is given freely to those who *give* it freely.

5) *Protection.* "And lead us not into temptation, but deliver us from evil." *(Matthew 6:13)* Jesus taught His disciples here to pray for total protection throughout their day.

6) *Praise.* "For thine is the kingdom, and the power, and the glory, forever. Amen." *(Matthew 6:13)* Jesus taught them to end this prayer time again with praise to their heavenly Father for who He is and the power that He releases into their life.

Double-Diamond *Principle*

When You Get In The Presence Of God, Your Best Ideas Will Surface.

Keep a prayer list. Set a special time each day, have a special place if possible.

Don't forget the *prayer of agreement;* "If two of you shall agree on earth as touching anything that they shall ask, it shall be done for them of my Father which is in heaven." *(Matthew 18:19)*

Jesus *prayed.*

That is why He was a Double-Diamond.

JESUS ROSE EARLY.

Champions seize their day.

Famous successful men usually get up early. Get an early start every day. You will be amazed how much you can accomplish when others are just beginning their day.

Jesus rose early. "And in the morning, rising up a great while before day, He went out, and departed in to a solitary place, and there prayed." *(Mark 1:35)* He consulted His Upline before He consulted anyone else. He pursued the influence of God. Early.

Joshua rose early. *(Joshua 6:12)*

Moses, the great deliverer of the Israelites, rose early. *(Exodus 8:20)* Abraham, the great Patriarch of the Jewish nation rose early. *(Genesis 19:27)*

You think more clearly in the morning. You can *focus.* Your day is *uncluttered.* As you accumulate the emotions and stress of others throughout the day, the quality of your work usually deteriorates.

Double-Diamond
Principle

**He Who Masters His Time,
Masters His Life.**

Your life style may be an exception to this rule. Many people work all night, and use their day time for sleeping. But, for the most part, most of us have discovered that the greatest hours of your day are early...uncluttered with the demands of others.

Jesus knew this.
That is why He was a Double-Diamond.

JESUS NEVER FELT HE HAD TO PROVE HIMSELF TO ANYONE.

You are already important.

You have nothing to prove to anyone. You are the offspring of a remarkable Creator. You have the mind of Christ. Your gifts and talents have been placed within you. *Find what they are. Celebrate them.* Find ways to use those gifts to improve others and help them achieve their dreams and goals.

But never, never, never exhaust and waste your energies trying to prove something to somebody else.

Worth must be discerned.

Jesus knew this. Satan tempted Him. "If thou be the son of God, command that these stones be made bread." *(Matthew 4:3)*

Jesus unstopped deaf ears. He opened blind eyes. He made the lame to walk. The dead were raised. Sinners were changed. Yet, the jeers of the doubters continued to scream into His ears at His crucifixion, "And saying, Thou that destroys the temple, and buildest it in three days, save thyself. If thou be the son of God, come down from the cross." *(Matthew 27:40)*

Double-Diamond Principle

Those Who Do Not Discern Your Worth Are Disqualified For Relationship.

What was Jesus' reaction? *He was confident of His worth.* He knew His purpose. *He refused to let the taunts of ignorant men change His plans.*

You are not responsible for anything but an honest effort to please God. *Keep focused.*

Jesus did.

That is why He was a Double-Diamond.

JESUS AVOIDED UNNECESSARY CONFRONTATIONS.

Stay away from unnecessary conflict.

It is exhausting. It is unproductive. Quarreling and arguing are a waste of time. Millions of dollars have been lost in negotiations because of an argumentative spirit. Warfare is costly. And nobody really wins.

Jesus knew the emptiness of anger. "And all they in the synagogue, when they heard these things, were filled with wrath, And rose up, and thrust Him out of the city, and led Him unto the brow of the hill whereon their city was built, that they might cast him down headlong. But He, passing through the midst of them, went His way." *(Luke 4:28-30)*

He went His way.

He did not oppose them. He did not fight them. *He had other plans.* He was about His Father's business. He focused on His own goals. "And came down to Capernaum, a city of Galilee, and taught them on the Sabbath days." *(Luke 4:31)*

He did not withdraw into depression. He did not enter into an unnecessary dialogue with them. He didn't cower in a corner of his parent's home. *He proceeded toward His mission and purpose.*

Double-Diamond Principle

**The Atmosphere You Permit Decides
The Product You Produce.**

Learn to keep your mouth shut. "Whoso keepeth his mouth and his tongue keepeth his soul from troubles." *(Proverbs 21:23)*

Jesus was a peacemaker.

That is why He was a Double-Diamond.

JESUS DELEGATED.

Know your limitations.

It is more productive to get ten men to work rather than you do the work of ten men. *Delegation is simply giving others necessary instructions and motivation to complete a particular task.* This takes time. It takes patience. But it is a long term benefit.

He commanded the multitudes. He instructed His disciples to have the people sit down. He distributed the loaves and fishes to His disciples for distribution. *(Matthew 14:19)* He sent His disciples to get a donkey. *(Matthew 21:2)* He gave instructions to a blind man to complete his healing. *(John 9:6-7)* He sent His disciples into cities to prepare for special meals. *(Mark 14:12-15)*

There are some important things you need to remember when you network with others:

1) Make a checklist of their exact responsibilities.

2) Carefully instruct them as to your exact expectations of them.

3) Give them the information and authority necessary to complete those tasks.

4) Set a specific deadline to finish the task.

5) Clearly show them how they will be rewarded for their effort.

Double-Diamond Principle

One Cannot Multiply.

Make the time to motivate and educate them as to your exact expectations. *Take the time to delegate.*

Jesus did.

That is why He was a Double-Diamond.

MASTER SECRET 51

JESUS CAREFULLY GUARDED HIS PERSONAL SCHEDULE.

Your daily agenda is your life.

You cannot save time. You cannot collect it. You cannot place it in a special bank vault. You are only permitted to spend it...wisely or foolishly. *You must do something with time.*

You will invest it or you will waste it.

Everyone has a hidden agenda. Those around you will be reaching to pull you "off course." You must be careful to *protect your list of priorities.*

Jesus did. There is a fascinating story in the Bible about it.

Lazarus, a close friend of Jesus, became sick. Mary and Martha, His two sisters sent word to Jesus to come. However, "When he had heard therefore that he was sick, he abode two days still in the same place where he was." Mary was upset, "Lord, if thou hast been here, my brother had not died." *(John 11:11-44)*

But Jesus had deliberately delayed His coming. He kept His own schedule. He protected His agenda. He did not allow emergencies of others to get Him off track. *He guarded His list of priorities.*

Double-Diamond Principle

Only You Know Your Priorities.

Make today count. Remember the 24 golden box cars on the track of success. *If you do not control what goes into each of your 24 golden box cars (hours) then somebody else will.*

Avoid distractions. Write your daily list of things to do. Protect your schedule. **This is your life.** Make it happen.

Jesus did.

That is why He was a Double-Diamond.

JESUS ASKED QUESTIONS TO ACCURATELY DETERMINE THE NEEDS AND DESIRES OF OTHERS.

Ask questions.

Interrogate your world. Insist on listening to the opinions and needs of others.

Almost nobody on earth listens to others. Nor questions them.

It is a master secret of success.

Jesus asked questions.

Once Simon Peter went fishing. He caught nothing. When the morning was come, Jesus was standing on the shore. Jesus calls out, "Children, have ye any meat?" *(John 21:5) He assumed nothing. He pursued information.*

Their answer was His entry point into their life. He had something they needed. He had information.

His question was a link to their future. It was the bridge for their relationship. He then instructed them, "Cast the net on the right side of the ship, and you shall find." *(John 21:6)*

Double-Diamond Principle

Information Is The Difference Between Your Present And Your Future.

Document the needs of others. Keep a Rolodex. Keep a notebook of their needs and desires. What are your customers' needs and desires. What are your customers' needs today? Are you *really listening* to them? Do they really feel you are listening to them? Most employees feel that their bosses really do not hear their complaints. Most employers feel that their employees do not interpret them correctly.

Jesus pursued information.

That is why He was a Double-Diamond.

JESUS ALWAYS ANSWERED TRUTHFULLY.

Be truthful.

Someone has said, "Tell the truth the first time, and you will never have to try and remember what you said." Truth will always outlast the storms of slander and false accusations.

Never misrepresent your product to a customer.

Carefully build and forge before your family the picture of total truth.

Nothing is more important in life than believability. When you lose that, you have lost the essence of favor, love, and success.

Jesus was Truth.

"I am the way, the truth, and the life: no man cometh unto the father, but by me." *(John 14:6)* His integrity intimidated hypocrites. They reacted to His purity. Honesty is a force. It will destroy mountains of prejudice and fear in a single blow. "God is not a man, that he should lie; neither the son of man, that he should repent: hath he said, and shall he not do it? or hath he spoken, and shall he not make it good?" *(Numbers 23:19)*

Double-Diamond Principle

Truth Is The Most Powerful Force On Earth Because It Cannot Be Changed.

Jesus was *always* truthful.

That is why He was a Double-Diamond.

JESUS STAYED IN THE CENTER OF HIS EXPERTISE.

Do what you do best.

What do you *love* to do? What do you *love* to talk about? What would you rather *hear* about than anything else on earth? What would you do with your life *if money was not a factor?* What do you do *best* of all?

Your joy is determined by doing what you love.

Jesus associated with fishermen. He talked to tax collectors. Doctors and lawyers and religious leaders were regularly in His life. *But He never wavered from His focus.* "How God anointed Jesus of Nazareth with the Holy Ghost and with power: who went about doing good, and healing all that were oppressed of the devil; for God was with him." *(Acts 10:38)*

He knew His mission.

He stayed focused. I really believe that *broken focus is the real reason men fail.*

Double-Diamond
Principle

The Only Reason Men Fail Is Broken Focus.

Some people take jobs because they are convenient or close to their home. One man told me that he had spent his entire life working on a job that made him miserable.

"Why have you worked there for twenty-seven years then?" I asked.

"It's only ten minutes from my house," he replied. "And in three years I will receive a gold watch. I don't want to leave too early and miss my gold watch."

What you love is a clue to your calling and talent.

Jesus knew this.

This is why He was a Double-Diamond.

JESUS ACCEPTED THE RESPONSIBILITY FOR THE MISTAKES OF HIS DOWN-LINE.

People make mistakes.

This is not a perfect world. Your business is not a perfect business. Your friendships are not flawless. Those who work with you will make errors.

Remember, *your down-line consists of those who receive your instructions.* You are mentoring them. They are in a process of growing. They are learning. They will stumble and make mistakes. Some of them will be costly.

I read an interesting story some years ago. An executive secretary to the president of a large corporation made a costly mistake. It cost the company $50,000.00. She was devastated and brought her letter of resignation to the president explaining, "I realize what a dumb thing I did. I am very sorry. I know that it cost the company $50,000.00. Here is my letter of resignation."

"Are you crazy?", he thundered. "I have been teaching you and educating you every week. Now, you have made a big mistake. I have just invested $50,000.00 in your education and you're going to leave. No, ma'am. You are not going to leave. You have cost me too much to lose my investment in you." She stayed and became an extraordinary executive.

Double-Diamond
Principle

Forgiveness Makes A Future Possible.

Peter denied the Lord. And yet Jesus lovingly said, "Simon, Simon, behold, satan hath desired to have you, that he may sift you as wheat: but I have prayed for thee, that thy faith fail not: and when thou art converted, strengthen thy brethren." *(Luke 22:31,32)*

Great leaders accept the responsibility for their troops. If you are going to have extraordinary success in your business, be strong and courageous enough to take the responsibility for the mistakes of those in the process of learning from you. Don't whine. Don't complain. Be strong.

Jesus was our supreme example.

That is why He was a Double-Diamond.

JESUS PURSUED THE MENTORSHIP OF MORE EXPERIENCED MEN.

Mentors are teachers in your life.

Your mentors are not perfect people. They simply have experienced life and are capable of transferring that knowledge into you. Your mentor can be older or younger than yourself. Your mentor is *anyone capable of growing and increasing your life.*

Show me your mentors, and I can predict your future. "A wise man will hear, and will increase learning; and a man of understanding shall attain unto wise counsels:" *(Proverbs 1:5)*

Jesus sought knowledge. When He was twelve, He pursued the teachers of His day. "And it came to pass, that after three days they found Him in the temple, sitting in the midst of the Doctors, both hearing them, and asking them questions." *(Luke 2:46)*

Ruth listened to the advice of Naomi. Esther listened to Mordecai. David sat at the feet of Samuel. Joshua received instructions from Moses. Timothy was mentored by Paul. Elisha ran to stay in the presence of Elijah.

Double-Diamond Principle

Diamonds Know Greatness When They Get In The Presence Of It.

"And when they saw Him, they were amazed: and His mother said unto Him, Son why hast thou thus dealt with us? behold, thy father and I have sought thee sorrowing. And He said unto them, How is it you sought me? wist ye not that I must be about my Father's business?" *(Luke 2:48,49)*

Solomon said, "Where no counsel is, the people fall: but in the multitude of counsellors there is safety." *(Proverbs 11:14)* "He that walketh with wise men shall be wise: but a companion of fools shall be destroyed." *(Proverbs 13:20)*

Listen to your up-line. Sit in their presence. Purchase their tapes. Absorb their books. *One sentence can be the golden door to the next season of your life.*

**The First Step Toward Success Is
The Willingness To Listen.**

Jesus was teachable.
That is why He was a Double-Diamond.

JESUS DID NOT PERMIT HIS DOWN-LINE TO SHOW DISRESPECT.

Never tolerate strife.

Strife will not go away voluntarily. You must confront it. *You will never correct what you are unwilling to confront.* Always name rebellion for what it is. Pinpoint rebellion. When there is a rebel in your company, discern it. *Mark those who create strife.* "Now I beseech you, brethren, mark them which cause divisions and offenses contrary to the doctrine which you have learned; and avoid them." *(Romans 16:17)*

Jesus loved people. He cherished hours with His disciples. He was a listener. He was gracious and humble. But, He was quite aware of something that every successful person should remember; *familiarity can often incubate disrespect.*

One day Peter began to feel extra comfortable with Jesus. Comfortable enough to correct Him. "Then Peter took him, and began to rebuke Him, saying, Be it far from thee, Lord: this shall not be unto thee." *(Matthew 16:22)*

Suddenly, the gentle and kind Jesus revealed His nature of steel. He was immovable. He was unshakable. And in a single stroke of communication, He stripped Peter of his cockiness. Peter had *presumed* on the relationship. Jesus had *never* given him the authority to correct Him. "But He turned, and said unto Peter, Get thee behind me, Satan; thou art an offense unto me: for thou savorest not the things that be of God, but those that be of men." *(Matthew 16:23)*

Double-Diamond
Principle

Never Complain About What You Permit.

Jesus did not tolerate disrespect.

You see, rebellion is contagious. One rebel can destroy thousands of people. *Confront those who cause contention.* Do not expect them to fade into the sunset. They never do.

Your business success depends on a peaceful and happy climate. You must constantly be aware of signs of discontent. Deal with it before it spreads like a virus throughout your organization.

One of the famous staff managers for a United States President says, "I manage by the acorn management philosophy. I look for problems when they are the size of an acorn. I refuse to watch them grow into oak trees."

People rarely respect and follow anyone they are capable of intimidating, dominating or manipulating.

Jesus knew this.

That is why He was a Double-Diamond.

JESUS UNDERSTOOD
SEED-FAITH.

Everything begins with a seed.

Someone plants a small acorn. It becomes the mighty oak tree. The small kernel of corn is planted. It produces two cornstalks. Each stalk produces two ears of corn. Each ear of corn contains over seven hundred kernels of corn. From that one small kernel of corn, a seed, 2800 more kernels are created.

Look at *seed as anything that can multiply and become more.* Love is a *Seed.* Money is a *Seed.* Everything you possess can be planted back into the world as a *seed.*

Your seed is anything that benefits another person.

Your harvest is anything that benefits you.

Seed-Faith simply means to plant *something you have,* like a seed, in faith, *for a specific harvest.*

Seed-Faith is using what you have been given, to create something else you have been promised. If you sow the seed of diligence on your job, your harvest will be a promotion. "The soul of the sluggard desireth, and hath nothing: but the soul of the diligent shall be made fat." *(Proverbs 13:4)* "He becometh poor that dealeth with a slack hand: but the hand of the diligent maketh rich." *(Proverbs 10:4)*

When you sow love into your family, you will reap love. When you sow finances into the work of God, you will reap financial blessings.

Double-Diamond
Principle

Seed-Faith Is Using What You Have To Create What You Want.

Jesus taught that giving was the beginning of blessings. "Give, and it shall be given unto you; good measure, pressed down, and shaken together, and running over, shall men give into your bosom. For with the same measure that ye mete withal it shall be measured to you again." *(Luke 6:38)*

This same scripture illustrates another incredible principle: *Whatever you are, you will create around you.* I am Irish. What will I create? Irishmen. What will a German create? Germans. What will a watermelon create? Watermelons. When you give, people around you start wanting to give to you.

It is simple, explosive and undeniable.

Double-Diamond
Principle

Giving Is The Only Proof You Have Conquered Greed.

Jesus taught the 100-fold principle. "And Jesus answered and said, Verily I say unto you, There is no man that hath left house, or brethren, or sisters, or father, or mother, or wife, or children, or lands, for my sake, and the gospel's, But he shall receive an hundredfold now in this time, houses, and brethren, and sisters, and mothers, and children, and lands, with persecutions; and in the world to come eternal life." *(Mark 10:29,30)*

Everything you have came from God. *Everything you will receive* in your future will come from God. He is your total Source for everything in your life. Never forget this.

He wants you to have His blessings. "For the Lord God is a sun and shield: the Lord will give grace and glory: no good thing will he withhold from them that walk uprightly." *(Psalms 84:11)* "Beloved, I wish above all things that thou mayest prosper and be in health, even as thy soul prospereth." *(III John 2)*

Double-Diamond
Principle

**When You Let Go Of What Is In Your Hand,
God Will Let Go Of What Is In His Hand For You.**

The secret of your future is determined by the seeds you sow today.

When you open your heart, God will open His windows. Never forget that ten-percent of your income is *Holy Seed.* It is called *"The Tithe."* "Bring ye all the tithes into the storehouse, that there may be meat in mine house, and prove me now herewith, saith the Lord of hosts, if I will not open you the windows of heaven, and pour you out a blessing, that there shall not be room enough to receive it. And I will rebuke the devourer for your sakes, and he shall not destroy the Fruits of your ground;" *(Malachi 3:8-12)*

You can give your way out of trouble. Your Seed can create any future you want. Remember, God has a Son, Jesus. He *sowed* Him in the earth, to produce a family. *Millions are born again because of His best Seed.*

Jesus knew this.

That is why He was a Double-Diamond.

ABOUT MIKE MURDOCK

➤ Has embraced his assignment to pursue...possess...and publish the Wisdom of God to heal the broken in his generation.

➤ Preached his first public sermon at the age of 8.

➤ Preached his first evangelistic crusade at the age of 15.

➤ Began full-time evangelism at the age of 19, in which he has continued for 28 years.

➤ Has traveled and spoken to more than 11,000 audiences in 36 countries, including East Africa, the Orient, and Europe.

➤ Receives more than 1,500 invitation each year to speak in churches, colleges, and business corporations.

➤ Noted author of 57 books, including the best sellers, "Wisdom for Winning", "Dream-Seeds", and "The Double Diamond Principle".

➤ Created the popular "Wisdom Topical Bible" series for Businessmen, Mothers, Fathers, Teenagers, and the One-Minute Pocket Bible.

➤ Has composed more than 1,200 songs such as "I Am Blessed", "You Can Make It", and "Jesus Just The Mention of Your Name", recorded by many gospel artists.

➤ He has released over 20 music albums as well, and the music video, "Going Back To The Word".

➤ Is a dynamic teacher having produced to date 21 Wisdom Teaching Tape series and 9 School of Wisdom videos.

➤ He has appeared often on TBN, CBN, and other television network programs.

➤ Is a Founding Trustee on the Board of Charismatic Bible Ministries.

➤ Is the Founder of the Wisdom Training Center, for the training of those entering the ministry.

➤ Has had more than 3,400 accept the call into full-time ministry under his ministry.

➤ Has a goal of establishing Wisdom Rooms in one million Christian homes.

➤ Has a weekly television program called "Wisdom for Crisis Times".

MY DECISION PAGE

May I Invite You To Make Jesus The Lord of Your Life?

The Bible says, "that if thou shalt confess with thy mouth the Lord Jesus Christ, and shalt believe in thine heart that God hath raised him from the dead, thou shalt be saved. For with the heart man believeth unto righteousness; and with the mouth confession is made unto salvation." (Romans 10:9,10)

To receive Jesus Christ as Lord and Saviour of your life, please pray this prayer from your heart today!

Dear Jesus,

I believe that You died for me and that You arose again on the third day. I confess to You that I am a sinner and that I need Your love and forgiveness. Come into my life, forgive my sins, and give me eternal life. I confess You now as my Saviour! I walk in your peace and joy from this day forward.

Signed _____

Date _____

☐ Yes, Mike, I have accepted Christ as my personal Saviour and would like to receive my personal gift copy of your book *31 Keys To A New Beginning.* (B 48) #DC10

Name _____

Address _____

City _____ State _____ Zip_____

Phone (   )_____ Birthdate _____

Occupation_____

YOUR LETTER IS VERY IMPORTANT TO ME

You are a special person to me, and I believe you are special to God. I want to help you in every way I can. Let me hear from you when you are facing spiritual needs or experiencing a conflict in your life, or if you just want to know that someone really cares. Write me. I will pray for your needs. And I will write you back something that I know will help you receive the miracle you need.

Mike, here are my special needs at this time:
-Please Print-

_____

_____

_____

_____

_____

_____

_____

_____

_____

_____

_____

_____

_____

Mail To:
MIKE MURDOCK
The Wisdom Center • P.O. Box 99 • Dallas, Texas 75221

WILL YOU BECOME A WISDOM KEY PARTNER?

1. TELEVISION - The Way Of The Winner, a nationally-syndicated weekly TV program features Mike Murdock's teaching and music.

2. WTC - Wisdom Training Center where Dr. Murdock trains those preparing for full-time ministry in a special 70 Hour Training Program.

3. MISSIONS - Recent overseas outreaches include crusades to East Africa, Brazil and Poland; 1,000 Young Minister's Handbooks sent to India to train nationals for ministry to their people..

4. MUSIC - Millions of people have been blessed by the anointed song-writing and singing talents of Mike Murdock, who has recorded over 20 highly-acclaimed albums.

5. LITERATURE - Best-selling books, teaching tapes and magazines proclaim the Wisdom of God.

6. CRUSADES - Multitudes are ministered to in crusades and seminars throughout America as Mike Murdock declares life-giving principles from God's Word.

7. SCHOOLS OF WISDOM - Each year Mike Murdock hosts Schools of Wisdom for those who want to personalized and advanced training for achieving their dreams and goals.

I want to personally invite you to be a part of this ministry!

WISDOM KEY PARTNERSHIP PLAN

Dear Partner,

God has brought us together! I love representing you as I spread His Wisdom in the world. Will you become my Faith-Partner? Your Seed is powerful. When you sow, three benefits are guaranteed:
PROTECTION *(Mal. 3:10-11),* FAVOR *(Luke 6:38),* FINANCIAL PROSPERITY *(Deut. 8:18). Please note the four levels as a monthly Wisdom Key Faith Partner. Complete the response sheet and rush it to me immediately. Then focus your expectations for the 100-fold return (Mark 10:30)!*

Your Faith Partner,

Mike Murdock

Yes, Mike, I want to be a Wisdom Key Partner with you. Please rush The Wisdom Key Partnership Pak to me today!

❑ **FOUNDATION PARTNER**...Yes, Mike, I want to be a Wisdom Key Foundation Partner. Enclosed is my first monthly Seed-Faith Promise of $15.

❑ **SEED-A-DAY**...Yes, Mike, I want to be a Wisdom Key Partner as a Seed-a-Day member. Enclosed is my first monthly Seed-Faith Promise of $30.

❑ **COVENANT OF BLESSING**...Yes, Mike, I want to be a Wisdom Key Partner as a Covenant of Blessing member. Enclosed is my first Seed-Faith Promise of $58.

❑ **THE SEVENTY**...Yes, Mike, I want to be a Wisdom Key Partner as member of The Seventy. Enclosed is my first monthly Seed-Faith Promise of $100.

TOTAL ENCLOSED $ _____ #DC10

Name _____

Address _____

City _____State _____Zip_____

Phone ( ) _____Birthday _____

Mail To:

MIKE MURDOCK

The Wisdom Center • P.O. Box 99 • Dallas, Texas 75221

WISDOM KEY PARTNERSHIP PAK

When you become a Wisdom Key Monthly Faith Partner or a part of The Seventy, you will receive our Partnership Pak which includes:

1. *Special Music Cassette*
2. *101 Wisdom Keys Book*
3. *Partnership Coupon Book*

Yes Mike! I Want To Be Your Partner!

❏ Enclosed is my best Seed-Faith Gift of $_____.

❏ I want to be a Wisdom Key Partner! Enclosed is my first Seed-Faith gift of $_____ for the first month.

❏ Please rush my special Partnership Pak. (#PP02)

Name _____

Address _____

City _____State _____Zip _____

Phone (   )_____

#DC10

Mail To:
MIKE MURDOCK
The Wisdom Center • P.O. Box 99 • Dallas, Texas 75221

4 POWER-PACKED TAPE SERIES BY MIKE MURDOCK

HOW TO WALK THROUGH FIRE

The 4 basic causes of conflict and how to react in a personal crisis, that are extremely helpful for those who are walking through the fires of marriage difficulty, divorce, depression, and financial adversity. (TS5)Six Tape Series

$30

THE ASSIGNMENT

Do you wonder why you are here? What are you tp do? These tapes will unlock the hidden treasures inside you to fulfill the *Assignment* God has called you to. 160 Wisdom Keys that can reveal the purpose of God. (TS22)Six Tape Series

$30

WOMEN THAT MEN CANNOT FORGET

Discover the success secrets of two of the most remarkable women in history...and how their secrets can help you achieve your dreams and goals! Both men and women will enjoy these wisdom secrets from the lives of Ruth and Esther. (TS31)Six Tape Series

$30

THE GRASSHOPPER COMPLEX

A must for those who need more self-confidence! It reveals the secrets of overcoming every giant you face in achieving your personal dreams and goals. (TS3)Six Tape Series

$30

Order All Four Series & Pay Only $100

6 Wisdom Books

WISDOM FOR CRISIS TIMES

Discover the Wisdom Keys to Dealing with tragedies, stress and times of crisis. secrets that will unlock the questions in the  right way to react in life situations. (Paperback)

(BK08) 118 Pages.....$7

THE DOUBLE DIAMOND PRINCIPLE

58 Master Secrets For Total Success, in the life of Jesus that will help you achieve your dreams and goals. (Paperback)

(BK71) 118 Pages.....$7

SEEDS OF WISDOM

One-Year Daily Devotional. A 374 page devotional with topics on dreams and goals, relationships, miracles, prosperity and more! (Paperback)

(BK02) 374 Pages.....$10

WISDOM FOR WINNING

The best-selling handbook for achieving success. If you desire to be successful and happy, this is the book for you! (Paperback)

(BK23) 280 Pages.....$9

ONE-YEAR TOPICAL BIBLE

A One-Minute reference Bible. 365 topics; spiritual, topical and easy to read. A collection of Scriptures relating to specific topics that challenge and concern you. (Paperback)

(BK03) 374 Pages.....$10

DREAM SEEDS

What do you dream of doing with you life? What would you attempt to do if you knew it was impossible to fail? This 118-page book helps you answer these questions and much more! (Paperback)

(BK20) 118 Pages.....$7

ORDER FORM

Item No.	Name of Item	Quantity	Price Per Item	Total
#TS22	The Assignment Tapes		30.00	$
#TS5	How To Walk Through Fire Tapes		30.00	$
#TS3	The Grasshopper Complex Tapes		30.00	$
#TS3	Women Men Cannot Forget Tapes		30.00	$
	All 4 Tape Series For $100.00			$
#BK20	Dream Seeds Book		7.00	$
#BK23	Wisdom For Winning Book		9.00	$
#BK20	Seeds of Wisdom Book (374 Pgs)		10.00	$
#BK71	Double Diamond Principle Book		7.00	$
#BK08	Wisdom For Crisis Times Book		7.00	$
#BK03	One Minute Topical Bible (374 Pgs)		10.00	$
SORRY NO C.O.D's		Add 10% For Shipping		$
		(Canada add 20%)		$
	Enclosed is my Seed-Faith Gift for Your Ministry.			$
#DC10		Total Amount Enclosed		$

Please Print

Name

Address

City

State _____ Zip

Phone(hm) _____ (wk)

☐ Check　☐ Money Order　☐ Cash

☐ Visa　☐ MasterCard　☐ AMEX

Signature_____

Card#

Expiration Date _____

☐ Send Free Catalog & Free Subscription To Newsletter *Wisdom Talk*

Mail To:
MIKE MURDOCK
The Wisdom Center • P.O. Box 99 • Dallas, Texas 75221

NOTES

NOTES

NOTES

NOTES

NOTES

NOTES

NOTES

NOTES

NOTES

NOTES